ACTIVATE GOD'S BLESSINGS
BLESS GOD BLESS YOU BLESS ME

FRANKLIN MARSHALL

Copyright 2020 by Franklin Marshall Ministries

All rights reserved. No part of this book may be used or reproduced in any manner whatsoever without written permission excerpt in the case of brief quotations embodied in critical articles or reviews.

Franklin Marshall Ministeries
P.O Box 2598
Santa Cruz, CA 95063
www.franklinmarshallministries@gmail.com
send feedback to email franklinmarshallministries@gmail.com

Printed in the United States of America

Library of Congress Cataloging-in-Publication data is available for this title.
ISBN: 978-1-893931-99-2

Copyediting, Proofreading, Cover design, Text design and composition by Franklin Marshall Ministries
Printed by Ingrams

Distributed by Franklin Marshall Ministries

To place order through www.franklinmarshallministries@gmail.com

Dedication

Firstly, I want to thank God for giving me the privilege to write this book. I already feel great enthusiasm because I know this book will help others tremendously. I would like to thank my beautiful mother, Hattie Marshall, who spent time reading bedtime Bible stories to me and my siblings every night. My mother prayed with us and my dad, Lenzie Marshall, who I always saw on his knees praying every morning by the woodstove. Also, my lovely wife – she spent countless hours working on this book with me. She would sometimes do edits while we spent get-away time in a hotel just to bring the book to standard. A strange man told me that I was going to publish my book in South Africa; perhaps, he was an angel from my hometown in Santa Cruz. However, I had previously tried to publish it but all attempts were futile. I would like to thank Victor Mathye and Jerry Mathye for being the inspiration to follow through in publishing the book after coming to South Africa.

I dedicate this book to Graciela Méndez, whom I saw Reading the Bible and saying her prayers daily; this portrayed true discipline and commitment to God. Lastly, I am grateful to God for blessing me with four beautiful children; this book is dedicated to them and everyone who inspired me including, Marisa, Dezmen, Zendrea, and Kevis Marshall.

Acknowledgement

Without the power and strength of God in our lives, there is absolutely nothing we can do. As a worship leader, I discovered the true meaning of prayer, which allowed me to exercise a divine process of seeking the Lord for His blessings on the people I worked with, in the ministry and congregation. God taught me how important it is to pray and what He will do as a result of our prayers. There have been times in my life where life was tough and God guided me through. The second section of this book. is the "*Rhythms, and Patterns to Success.*" Here, we learn that prayer without some effort behind is futile. In the scripture it says « faith without works is dead! » In the latter part of this book, God showed me the importance of reaching out in an intentional way to share His gospel, spreading it on minds and hearts at all times to the glory of God.

Foreword

"I believe this book can be used for Spiritual direction and works of mercy. Invested with good text for clarifying thought with works/gospel."
— Director of Saint Frances Soup Kitchen, Richard Crowe,

"I appreciate that the gospel is at the heart of it. It seems to be put together well - gives lots of ideas."
— Calvary Chapel of Monterey Pastor Bill Holderage

"Equipped with fun ideas for youth and young adults. This book guides the reader step by step to share his/her faith and enjoy the blessings in return!"
— Principal of Virgial Hausalt Academy Christian School Larry Balew

"It is an excellent tool for:
1. Determining what ministries and outreaches the Lord is calling Particular individuals; congregations to.
2. Planning of more specific steps to fulfill the calling(s)
3. Scheduling steps for development and timing for outreaches."
— Staff of Bethany Bible College and Pastor of An Assembly of God Church J. Richard Tennesen

Preface

When I think about the three areas of this book, it has something for everyone, especially believers in Christ. There are three sections to this book that are extremely vital. Prayer shows how small of a prayer we can pray and God will hear it and listen to the large needs that we have when we pray. There are times when we feel like praying alone. This is the real key to accomplishing life's goals. The Rhythm And Patterns to Success section of this book talks about prayer, in action which is faith without works is dead and is so important. For instance, if you want your degree from a University then you must study hard. You need to go to class, take tests, and pass to get your degree. While, we are in school, we may pray and hope we make good grades, but prayer alone cannot get you good grades. You have to put action to it and look at everything in life in this way. In Isaiah 58, God inspired me to write about simple things that we can do daily to reach out to share his love with our sphere of influence. There are many simple ideas/concepts revealed in the outreach section. However keep in mind that nothing is too small when sharing the love of Christ Jesus.

Author's Note

A Tool For Spiritual, Personal, And Church Growth

I am eternally grateful to God, who has given me the privilege to put together this book. Activate God's Blessings is a combination of three small booklets that I have worked on at different times throughout the years. The first section of the book, which deals with prayers, was written closer to the year 2016. The second section, which is the personal development, was written in 1997, while the outreach book section, which is the last part of the booklet, was also written around 2000 through the insight given to me by God. Each of these booklets ended up having 30 days of inspirational information that will ultimately transform your life. So, why this book? The need to have a single comprehensive book made me entertain the idea of putting the three booklets together. I aim to utilize this ministry to encourage, lift in prayer, and reach out to help those whose hope and aspiration is in the Lord. My sincere desire is that God would move upon your heart to seek him so that your life would be enhanced as you use the personal development skills, and many souls would be won to Christ through your love and concern for others in the outreach section.

Contents

Section One

ACTIVATE GOD'S BLESSINGS THROUGH PRAYER

What is Activating God's Blessings? 1
Examples of answered Prayers 2
What happens when you spend real time with God? 3
What can or do we pray for? 4
Praying together as Couples, Children, and Groups 4
What are the Mechanics and the DNA of Prayer? 5
What happens in heaven and on earth when we pray? 5
Can Prayer affect our faith? 6
Prayer can give you peace and comfort 6
Prayer and Fasting 7
Pray your Way to Breakthrough 8
    1. Prayer for Our Pets 8
    2. Prayer for the Family 9
    3. Prayer for Our Body 10
    4. Prayer for Our Nation 11
    5. Prayer for Mental And Spiritual Enlightenment 11
    6. Prayer for Favor 12
    7. Prayer for Jobs 13
    8. Prayer for Shelter 14
    9. Prayer for Mercy during the Time of Coronavirus Pandemic 14

10. Prayer for Unity 15
11. Prayer for the Animals on Earth and in the Sea 16
12. Prayer for Favor in the Earth, in the Air and in the Water 17
13. Prayer for Our Neighborhoods 18
14. Prayer for Peace in the Parks and Recreational Areas 19
15. Prayer for Direction During Finance 20
16. Prayer for Vitality of Health 20
17. Prayer for Salvation 21
18. Prayer for Intimate Relationship with God 21
19. Prayer against Addiction 21
20. Prayer for Absolute Peace 22
21. Prayer for Heavenly Provision 22
22. Prayer for Divine Direction 23
23. Prayer for Faith in God 23
24. Prayer for Strength in the Lord 23
25. Prayer for Our Institutions 24
26. Prayer for Our Industries 24
27. Prayer for Our Governors and Mayors in the Helm of Affairs . 25
28. Prayer for Our States and Cities 25
29. Prayer for Our Nation's Leaders 26
30. Prayer for Money 26
31. Prayer for Money and Wise Investments 27

Section Two

PERSONAL DEVELOPMENT

Seeking Divine Mentorship 30
The Role Of Personal Development In Your Life As A Christian 32
Using Jesus As Our Model For Personal Development 33
Rhythm and Patterns to Personal Development 36
The 30 days Daily Rhythm Activities Toward Your
   Personal Development 39

DAY 1: VISUALIZE WHO YOU WANT TO BE 39
DAY 2: SET GOALS 39
DAY 3: CREATE A CREATIVE ENVIRONMENT 40
DAY 4: CREATE A PLAN AND WRITE IT DOWN 41
DAY 5: FIND YOUR RHYTHMS AND PATTERNS 42
DAY 6: GET AN ATTITUDE — A POSITIVE ONE 43
DAY 7: BUILD FAITH AND COMMITMENT 43
DAY 8: KNOWING YOU CAN CHANGE BRINGS FREEDOM 44
DAY 9: BANISH FEAR BY BEING IN THE PRESENT 45
DAY 10: KNOW THAT AN UNSEEN POWER IS THERE TO HELP YOU 46
DAY 11: LOVE AND LIVE LIFE — GIVE A SMILE AWAY 46
DAY 12: PRACTICE LISTENING AS YOU WOULD PRACTICE A SPORT 47
DAY 13: WHAT YOU GIVE IN A RELATIONSHIP YOU WILL RECEIVE 48
DAY 14: SHARE YOUR IDEAS WITH SUPPORTIVE PEOPLE 49
DAY 15: FIND A TRUE MENTOR 50
DAY 16: TAKE A GOOD LOOK AT YOURSELF 50
DAY 17: THE ELECTRICITY OF TEAMWORK 51
DAY 18: NETWORKING'S THE WAY TO GO 52
DAY 19: CREATE HARMONY — BANISH STRESS 52
DAY 20: EXERCISE 53
DAY 21: MAKING OPPORTUNITIES OUT OF CRISIS 54
DAY 22: GROW INTELLECTUALLY AND SPIRITUALLY 54
DAY 23: INCORPORATE CHARITY IN YOUR LIFE 55
DAY 24: YOU ARE A VALUED EMPLOYEE 56
DAY 25: CREATE A STUDY HOUR 57
DAY 26: PRACTICE AND REHEARSE 58
DAY 27: CHOOSE YOUR WORDS WISELY 58

DAY 28: MAKE DECISIONS, TRUST INTUITION 59
DAY 29: FISCAL RESPONSIBILITY 60
DAY 30: YOU ARE WHAT YOU THINK................................61
Setting Goals for Personal Development 62

Section Three
ACTIVATE GOD'S BLESSINGS THROUGH OUTREACH

Understanding The Concept Of Blessing 70
   1. Acknowledge God As The Source Of All Blessings................... 70
   2. Seize the choice to be blessed. 71
   3. Following His Commandments Leads To Blessings 71
How Giving Relates To God's Will 72
Helping With The Newborn As An Outreach 74
Helping The Homeless As An Outreach 76
Helping The Widows As An Outreach 78
Helping With Food As An Outreach 79
Helping With Tutoring and Developing Personal
   Skills As An Outreach... 81
Helping Public Schools & College As An Outreach 82
Helping The Elderly As An Outreach 84
Helping On The Telephone As An Outreach 85
Helping Those In Grief As An Outreach 86
Helping With Job/Employee As An Outreach 87
Helping With Those in Businesses As An Outreach 89
Helping With Those in Prison/Jail As An Outreach 90
Helping With People Living on the Street As An Outreach 91
Helping With Those in Your Neighborhood As An Outreach 93
Helping With The Ministry Of Writing As An Outreach 94
Helping Through Sports As An Outreach 95
Helping Through Music As An Outreach... 96

Helping Through the Media As An Outreach 98
Helping Through The Internet As An Outreach 99
Helping Those With Health Issues As An Outreach 100
Helping With Visiting The Sick As An Outreach 101
Helping With The Handicapped As An Outreach 103
Helping Those With Substance Abuse As An Outreach 104
Helping With Those in Shelters As An Outreach 105
Helping With Children As An Outreach 107
Helping Relatives As An Outreach 108
Helping The Convalescent & Hospitals As An Outreach 109
Helping With Pregnant Teens As An Outreach 110
Helping With Parent Development As An Outreach 112
Helping With The Fatherless/Motherless As An Outreach 113

Conclusion – We Are Called For Good Works 115
Community Outreach Organizations to Work With 121
Outreach Contact List 123
Directory of Local Churches 124
Prayer Requests 125
How to guide people in Prayer when they are ready to accept Christ. 126
Useful Scriptures for Outreach 129
Personal Outreach Timeline Community Needs 139

Section One

ACTIVATE GOD'S BLESSINGS THROUGH PRAYER

What is Activating God's Blessings?

When we think about blessings, we think of receiving something of value. When we think of blessing God, we think of giving Him our best praise, worship, and obedience. When we think about blessing others, we look at it in the same way, we want to give them something that would bring relief to them somehow. It will give us a sense of gratitude. What I would like to deal with in this book are these three areas of blessings. Blessing God, the blessing for yourself, and blessing others. The Bible says, "…for your Father knows what you need before you ask him" (Matthew 6:8). Another scripture says, "You do not have because you do not ask God" (James 4:2). I am reminded of one more scripture that I enjoy which is, "…so faith without deeds is dead" (James 2:26). Many scriptures deal with our benevolence and offering to God, and an explanation of how He can bless us in return from our heart of giving Him our gifts.

When I think about activating God's blessings, I love the scriptures that say, "we have not because we ask not,» and "faith without works is dead," those two scriptures are very significant. They give us a clear description of how God operates. He is there for us with blessings and takes care of our needs. However, He requires something from us. I feel that prayer is such an important part of our daily living, whenever we have anything to do, prayer should be the first thing we focus on because God's direction is essential to a successful life. From health, relationships, finances, and the environment we live in. Our surroundings in every way are dependent upon the blessings we receive from God, and as we come before Him, we can walk in His ways. When we hear from Him, when we talk to Him, then we'll be able to understand His voice, and we can walk and be led by His voice.

When I think about enhancing our lives and personal development, there is a process involved. If you want to go to school and get a degree, you have to study. If you want to lose weight, you have to regulate your diet and do some form of exercise. If you want to grow spiritually, you have to spend time reading the Bible and praying. And that's the reason I like, "Faith without works is dead." When I think about reaching out to others, I know it is a mandate from God to reach out and be a blessing to those around us. Widows, orphans, the hungry, and the sick. Isaiah 58 is the scripture and the chapter that God gave me, this verse of the scripture inspired me to put this section together on reaching out to people, giving them a helping hand. It is a mandate from God that if we do these things, He would shine His light upon us and bless us.

Examples of answered Prayers

I have prayed, written down prayers, and repeatedly prayed for something that I wanted. Sometimes, those prayers were answered, and some prayers are still awaiting an answer from God. Maybe it's for a good reason, and that reason is best known to God because He does things at His appointed time. If I love God and God loves me, maybe it's not the right time for those things to come about. I've prayed for people as well as certain things and seen God move. I have a friend that wanted to get married; we prayed for her to get married. She ended up getting married after she was over 60. She was always in agony that she didn't have a husband; she is now happily married. I prayed for my business in the past, that it would become very successful. I have had some successes, and I have had some failures. I often wonder why I didn't have all the successes after spending so much time in prayer. When I look back, I can see God's hand and how He has been guiding me in a specific direction that was more in line with His will. I remember praying for a car diligently, wanting a new car, and it seems that it took so long to get a new car. It came at a point where I was not really focused on getting a new car, but I can see it came at the perfect time.

What happens when you spend real time with God?

The effect of prayer is so broad, vast, valuable, and simple even to the point where we don't take advantage of the benefits and the attributes that come from prayer. The scripture Matthew 17:21 says, « some things only come about by prayer and fasting. » I remembered as a worship leader at Calvary Chapel Church, I decided to experiment with prayer and fasting on a Saturday before I went to church. I spent all day and even late into the night on my knees, praying and fasting just to see what would happen. On Sunday morning worship service, when the service started, it was as if I was not even trying; people were so happy, rejoicing, singing, and clapping. They were smiling at each other. It was just overwhelming to see the reaction of the congregation; it showed me at that point that there was a real breakthrough. Something significant happened with all of the prayer and fasting. I saw God's hand upon the people as I did my part leading worship, God manifested Himself 1000 times more, reaching out and blessing the congregation.

What can or do we pray for?

When I was in the ministry as a young person in Calvary Chapel Church leading worship, I would pray and seek God for an outpouring of the Holy Spirit upon the congregation. I would pray for various needs, finances, health, relatives, and a wife. I never considered praying for the environment around me. I included this prayer into the book. There are various areas that we can pray for, not only pray for what God can give us. We can give praises for all of these areas, the trees, the sky, the clouds, the moon, and the stars. We can praise God for the mountains, the oceans, the rivers, the streams, the atmosphere, and our surroundings. There's an unlimited number of things that we can praise God for, and we can pray for these things as directed by the Holy Spirit. We can pray for these things in a way to sustain our environment, to bless our sea life, and to bless our pets. Sometimes we don't consider praying for these things because they seem so out of touch, removed from our everyday prayer.

Praying together as Couples, Children, and Groups

One of the things that I constantly did after becoming a Christian was that I prayed a lot. When I met my wife while we were dating, we ensured that the habit of constant prayer was our daily routine. We kept prayer consistently in our everyday life. Even when we were apart physically, we would call each other and pray together on the phone. Sometimes, my wife would feel elated that we have been together for the many years that we've been married. She feels like it's because of one thing or another, but one of the things that I always remind her of is that prayer had played a key role in sustaining our marriage. God is the cause of our being together and staying together. God is the one that has given us the motivation and the incentive to pray.

What are the Mechanics and the DNA of Prayer?

What happens when we pray? What kind of prayers should we pray? How do we pray to touch God's heart, and have Him listen to us and answer our prayers? An example of this type of prayer can be seen in the book of Daniel chapter 10; Daniel was praying and fasting for 21 days. The angel Gabriel came to Daniel after 21 days and explained to Daniel that he had trouble getting through to God because of a war that was taking place in the heavens over Persia. This is one of the examples of some things that go on in the heavens, which sometimes prevent some of our prayers from being heard or answered. Daniel got his answer after 21 days. There is a spiritual warfare taking place around us on earth and in the heavens continuously. And that is why we have Jesus, who is our advocate between the Father and us, and prayer is the key that moves the heavenly host to act on our behalf.

What happens in heaven and on earth when we pray?

There's a scripture that says God longs to give good gifts to His children, and He is waiting to bless us. There are mechanisms and ways that I've talked about earlier on how we can receive God's blessings. We need to walk upright before Him. There are several criteria that God asks of us to bless us. I mentioned Isaiah 58, reaching out to the orphans, the homeless, the widows, and the sick. God said that He would shine His light upon us like the noonday sun. There is a scripture that says, "Give, and it will be given to you. A good measure, pressed down, shaken together and running over, will be poured into your lap. For with the measure you use, it will be measured to you" (Luke 6:38). The Bible says, "Take delight in the Lord, and He will give you the desires of your heart," (Psalms 37:4). The scriptures also say that God's word is like a medicine to us. If we meditate on it day and night, "That person is like a tree planted by the streams, which yields its fruit in season and whose leaf does not wither-whatever they do prospers," (Psalms 1:2-3). There's so much value in prayer and being close to God.

Can Prayer affect our faith?

There's a scripture that says if we have the faith like the size of a mustard seed, "You can say to this mountain, 'Move from here to there' and it will move. Nothing will be impossible for you," (Matthew 17:20). This seems like such a small amount of faith, but if we have that kind of faith, we can do miracles. I've seen that my faith has become immovable through prayer, and yours can be also if you spend time with God. When I pray, and I know that I've prayed aligned with God's word, I have confidence that God is going to work things out. He has never failed me. I would plead with the Lord seeking His face and going out to work or any endeavor that I've prayed about. I've seen God's hand move on my behalf in relation to a specific issue that I have been praying about. I've seen miracles taking place as a result of my communion with God.

Prayer can give you peace and comfort

When we pray, there is a miracle that happens within us physiologically. We become much more peaceful; we are much more in tune with things around us and God's voice when we spend time with Him. Prayer should be a continuous spiritual activity throughout the day. We should always be in the spirit of prayer. The Bible says to pray without ceasing, and that literally means looking up to God in our hearts with the anticipation of hearing the quietness of His voice. In everything that we do, be it politics, business, relationships, and the environment. We need to continually have a mind of prayer, and a heart of communion with God. Looking up to God, speaking to Him without opening our mouths. Having prayers in our hearts and our subconscious mind.

Prayer and Fasting

When I was a kid, my dad would gather the whole family around to read scriptures and lead us in prayer. When I became a father and had children, I followed the same patterns. I would gather my family to pray; I would also call on the family sometimes to engage in fasting. While there are many different types of fast, most of the time with the children, we would fast from watching television. I remember we were once on a 30 day fast completely away from watching TV and what happened? A Miracle happened. I was in a coffee shop working on the outreach part of this book. A lady came up to me and asked me what I was doing. I told her that I was working on a life-changing book. She gave me her phone number and told me if I needed any help ever to let her know, she was a photographer.

This same lady came to me the following week; I saw her in front of a store on the street. She insisted again that she would like to help. I told her I had a children's program that I was working on, which was much more developed than the outreach book. She insisted that she would like to be a part of the outreach program. She wanted to know how she could help. I told her I was working on developing a prototype. She said, "I will help you fund it. How much do you need?" I told her it would be around $1000 and she told me that she would give me $2000. I was left in complete shock because she had only just met me. The following week she gave me $2000 in cash in an envelope. Once I had a prototype of the book, I showed it to her. She was so excited about it, to the extent she wanted to give me more money. She asked me what the next level I wanted to go to with the outreach book. I told her I didn't know, I needed several things completed, she took me to the bank. I waited for a few minutes, and she came back from the teller window with 90 hundred-dollar bills giving me $9000 dollars. I took this money home and gathered the family, we sat around with the television off. I reminded the children that we had been fasting and praying for God's blessings just to give them a sense of what God can do when we pray and fast. My take away lesson is that prayer is so simple yet so necessary, and it can change the world and even the course of history. The Bible says that the heart of the king is in the hands of the Lord; let us always pray and patiently wait until God hears our voice.

Pray your Way to Breakthrough

This aspect of the book contains specific prayer requests necessary to usher you to your divine breakthrough. We, as Christians, must cultivate the habit of opening our mouths in prayer and supplication; we must call on God for assistance. It is evident that He is willing to hear us in our time of distress. The prayer requests cover all areas of our lives, and what we need for Him to listen to us is to employ our faith as we call on Him.

1. Prayer for Our Pets

God, you are the creator of all things. You made the birds of the heavens; the fish of the deep; the animals on earth and the animals for whom we care. Lord, we know that you glory in your whole creation, and you made it all, and it is good.

Father, it's a true delight that you've given us precious animals to care for, and even animals who care for us, and we can be friends with them. Dear God, it seems like such a small thing to pray, as we look upon our pets, these are your creations, You love them, You have blessed them, and we want to be a blessing to them.

Father, give us compassion for our small and large pets. Oh Lord, I pray your blessings would be upon our pets. Provide them good health and a long life. I pray for wisdom on how to care for our pets with wisdom from above. God, we know you love all of your creation, and this is just a small fraction of your extended hand of mercy.

We pray for Your wisdom and grace. Heavenly Father, I pray for peace upon our pets. I pray for a gentle spirit upon our pets. I pray for our companionship and enjoyment together and that we'll be a blessing to one another. Let all of Your pets that are in homes, across this nation, be blessed. Heavenly Father, we offer up all of the abused animals throughout this nation and in the world. We pray for Your grace and mercy upon them. Lord God, I pray You will keep all pets from sickness and disease. Keep them strong with healthy teeth and bodies; give us wisdom how to care for Your pets, let Your grace be upon our unity as pet and caretakers. We seek Your guidance and blessings. We ask for Your grace to abound in Jesus' name, Amen.

2. Prayer for the Family

God, You are so awesome; You deserve the ultimate praise. I will lift my voice and sing Your glorious praise forever. I will stretch my hands to You, Oh God. On every occasion, I will seek Your favor, and delight in Your grace. You shine so brightly for everyone to see Your glory. It is revealed for all eternity. With all my soul, I lift You up so high.

I glory in Your name, without a doubt, and without any shame. You alone are the Awesome God. You are the great I AM; You are the deliverer. You keep my life and sustain my family. You have all power in Your hands. Father in heaven, You made the family, You made man and woman; You gave children; You blessed the baron and gave children to fathers and mothers, You created the family. You desire for them to serve You, God.

We pray for our family and that Your blessings would rest upon families throughout this nation. We pray for Your anointing to keep us healthy. Bless us in every way on our jobs, upon our health, upon our children's children and future generations that we will endeavor to do Your will that Your name may continue in our families forever, Oh God.

Dear God, I pray for all of my family members to come to an understanding and love for You, that they may know and experience Your love the way I do. Give me wisdom, dear God, how to minister to them, how to show them who You are. I pray that You will give them openness and a longing for that void in their hearts to be filled. Lord. You know what's in their hearts. Father, You know which family members to whom You wish to speak. God, I pray You will have mercy on my family: allow them to come to You with outstretched arms. Give me the grace not to be judgmental but to have the love and patience so their lives may grow in Your grace. Lord, I thank You for giving me a desire to pray for my family. I trust You, Oh God, that You will bring them to Yourself that You may be glorified in every way in Jesus' name, Amen.

3. Prayer for Our Body

God, You are so High, and You can reach below; we thank You, Oh God, and we pray for Your blessings to flow upon our life: blessings upon my body for healing and restoration. Dear God, give me the wisdom and understanding of how to take care of my health in every way. You said, "We have not because we ask not," You also said, "faith without works is dead." God, give me a balance in faith and works. There is nothing I can do without You; without Your inspiration, without Your life-giving hands. God, I honor You; I trust in You, Oh God. Lord, You are the Almighty, and there is none higher than You. You created the world and all that is in it. I offer You my life, my body, my soul, and everything within me. Let all that I am, be a blessing and pleasing to You in every way, in Jesus' name, Amen.

4. Prayer for Our Nation

I've seen Your majesty even in the black of night, Oh God. I see Your glory in the heavens and all the earth. Your splendor is revealed in all living things. God Your glory is a delight in every way. Because You are all-powerful, I acknowledge that Your power gives life, salvation and restoration to all. Heavenly Father, in Your word You, said that by Your stripes we are healed. We cry out to You God for Your mercy, for Your tender grace upon the people of our nations. Restore us oh holy one, give us health in our bodies, our minds and spirit. Restore us now almighty God, in every corner of our nations, give us a yearning, a longing, and an outpouring of Your Spirit. We are deficient in spiritual rejuvenation; only You oh God can give an empowering, outpouring of the spirit like the days of Pentecost. We cry out to You, oh dear God, that You will be mindful of us Your people. Shower down upon us Your grace, shower down upon us Your mercy, fill our cups Lord as the body of Christ, let it overflow that our nations and the world will see You and You will be exalted in the earth through Your people, in Jesus' name, Amen.

5. Prayer for Mental And Spiritual Enlightenment

God, You have given us so much, and with the graciousness, You have shown, I honor and glorify Your name forever. You said in Your word, "So as a man thinks so is, he." God, You have sent Your Son, Jesus Christ, here on earth to experience what we go through. You understand every element of human agony. You feel every level of sensitivity we encounter. God, there are those who experience deficiencies of the mind daily. God, we pray for healing; we pray for restoration; we pray for the right person or persons to be the inspiration for those who require mental and spiritual enlightenment.

God, many times people are restricted from achieving their highest potential because of mental and emotional stress. We pray You will minister to their minds and give them an open-heart; give them a teachable spirit to hear what You have to say to them through Your servants. Oh God, we pray You will break down the walls and barriers, which these principalities have placed in the hearts and the minds of Your people. God, through our prayers, You said that we have power. You said whatever we lose on earth will be loosed in heaven, so we pray the prayer of freedom and deliverance for Your people. We offer up prayers for anyone experiencing depression or any level of misfortune. Restore them mentally, restore them spiritually, bless them, and keep them. We pray this in Jesus' name, Amen

6. Prayer for Favor

You alone, oh Lord, are glorious. You alone are victorious. You said, "The heart of the King is in Your hand." God, we thank You that we can trust You; we can believe in You; we can express our gratitude to You because You are so great. There is none like unto You, oh God. You made the heavens and the earth. You made the moon the stars and everything that dwells on the earth. You are so awesome in all of Your ways, oh God. Thank You, Lord God, for the breath I breathe. Thank You, oh God, for the words that I can speak to You glory and honor. May the praise be yours forever.

Most Righteous God, You can harden hearts; You can make them soft; You can speak to the highest of the high and those who are lowly. We, oh God, are totally dependent on You for Your grace and Your mercy. We do not trust in man but in You alone. We do not believe a decision made in our favor is strictly from man, but rather, it is from You. Your angels and the Holy Spirit have intervened on our behalf. As we acknowledge, we are not in control of our destiny; we cry out to You, Oh God, for Your blessings. We cry out for Your favor upon our decision and interaction with those with whom we are in contact. When we receive favor, Oh God, we know we did not receive it on our own. You are the giver of good gifts. You are the creator of the world. You are our life and salvation. We thank You for Your gift, and we honor You for Your help in Jesus' name, Amen.

7. Prayer for Jobs

Father God, we delight in You today. We magnify and praise Your greatness. You are exalted, Oh God. You are exalted in the heavens; You are exalted in Your creation; You are exalted in all of Your handiwork. You oh God are the Most High in the heavens. You promised us man would work by the sweat of his brow. We thank You for the ability to work. We thank You for the willingness to work. We pray, Dear Father in heaven that You will open doors for those who are less fortunate in these times.

Some are unemployed; they are not able to find a job; thus, these people find it difficult to meet their needs. I pray, Oh Most Holy and Awesome God, that You will shine Your blessings upon those who are in need of employment. I pray, Oh Dear God, You will give jobs, innovation, and creativity to start their own business. I pray that You will take away any fear or doubt in the minds of those who are in need of work. Give them the heart to believe and to receive Your blessings. Give them an outlook of great possibilities for there is no lack in Your gifts.

Let the weak say, "I am strong. Let the poor say, I am rich for what the Lord has done for me." Give them faith, for Your word says, "Faith is the substance of things hoped for and the evidence of things not seen." Lord give them a renewed heart and mind, with new words on their tongues. Oh Lord God, we magnify Your name; we glorify Your name, and we thank You for Your blessings. Thank You, Oh God, for what You have done. We thank You, Oh God, for we have no doubt You will fulfill Your promise. We honor You; we glory in You, and we say, "You are an awesome God" in Jesus' name, Amen.

8. Prayer for Shelter

Most Righteous God and Holy Father, we know You are High and lifted up. You can look down into the deepest ocean, and at the same time, see the most elevated planet. Your word said You care for the birds of the field and all of the animals. We should not worry about needs because You will take care of them. Father, I pray that You will give favor to those who are homeless and need a place to stay. Give us the courage to be instruments for Your Glory, making sure that Your Name is honored in all that we do. When we see those less fortunate, who need shelter, need food, let us be mindful of all that You've done for us, and how we need to spread Your love when reaching out to others. We draw upon Your strength. We believe by faith, and we receive all You have for us. In Your creation, we will be victorious; we will be courageous; we will let the world know that You are the living God. We will proclaim Your majestic power and love throughout the world. We accept and receive Your blessings, and Your Grace will flow through us like a mighty river and rushing mighty wind. We will bless and not restrain. We will proclaim and not hold back. We will declare, "This is the day that the Lord has made; we shall rejoice and be glad in it." We honor You Most Holy and High God. We bless You from the depth of our hearts; we thank You for Your power and Your blessings on those less fortunate. We receive all of Your blessings in Jesus' Name, Amen.

9. Prayer for Mercy during the Time of Coronavirus Pandemic

Your mercy is new every morning. Great is Your love and Your salvation. God, thank You for this wonderful day. You have given us so much, and we are grateful. You have given us the ability to communicate with You. We have our right mind with the right heart, which is from You, to pray the prayers of faith; to believe in Your word; to hope in Your salvation. We are continuously in awe of Your great love You have for humanity. We call upon You, Oh God, of heaven and earth, that You will look down upon Your people: the poor, the downtrodden, the outcast and those who have suffered from the Coronavirus and any other pandemic we may face. You know their needs before we even bring them up. You have given us the task as Your creation, here on earth, to petition You for those who are less fortunate for issues surrounding us. I am grateful, Oh God, that I can pray and believe just as Your word has said, "if we have faith the size of a mustard seed, we can say to a mountain be removed, and it will happen." So I bring the poor, weak, and sick from Coronavirus and other worldwide pandemics before You, to ask You for Your blessings; Your grace; Your outpouring love and charity to those in need. I know Oh God we are Your instruments; Your creations to be used by You, to fulfill Your desire, to reach out and touch someone in need. Oh God of heaven we petition You to use us, to work through us. Give us a willing heart; give us the words; give us Your blessings so that we may share them with those who are in need.

10. Prayer for Unity

God, You said that You are not the author of confusion, but You are the God of peace, righteousness, and everything good. I honor You for Your righteousness; I honor You for Your grace; Your love and Your never-ending delight. Lord God, I bring my heart to You; my song, and my dance. I will glory in You always. I will have laughter, joy, jubilance, and everlasting hope in You. God, we have had the architect of Satan upon this earth working day and night to divide us, to keep us confused and distracted in so many ways. As we acknowledge this today, we bring confusion before Your throne, misguided intention that has maliciously destroyed so many lives. God, we pray for all of these things.

Oh Lord God of heaven and earth, we pray for a new birth of understanding and blessings. We pray for Your unity; we pray for Your grace; we trust You, Oh God, for the hope that is in You. There can be no peace nor unity without Your grace; therefore, we pray, Oh, heavenly Father, that Your mercy will prevail. Give our hearts yearning for Your grace, Your unity, and Your peace. Ignite our sensitivity for the hope of joy, peace, unity, and enlightenment. Let Your grace Oh God rain upon us like a mighty wind and the largest tsunami of Your Holy Spirit. Dear God, we stand here with open arms, open hearts, opened lives to be Your vessels. May we do Your will to bring Your glory, Your peace, and Your unity upon this earth. We pray the prayer of faith; we pray the prayer of hope, thanksgiving, and we expect not because of our doing, but because we want to do it out of obedience to You Oh God. To honor You and to glorify Your Name. Bring unity Oh Lord God Almighty. Bring unity King of all Kings and Lord of Lords, give us unity we pray in Jesus' Name, Amen.

11. Prayer for the Animals on Earth and in the Sea

The whales, the birds, the fish of all types, the great octopus, the muscle, clams, oysters, the cows, the donkeys, the horses, the buffalos, the elks; the elephants, the giraffes, the tigers, the lions, the rhinoceros, the apes, the monkeys, the alligators, the crocodiles, the lizards and many more are all part of Your glory upon this earth. You, Oh God, are the God of all Gods. God, we have seen mass destruction upon this earth as a result of Your animals dying. God, You know the reason — we are baffled and confused at such great losses that we have encountered here on earth. God, we pray and stand in the gap for Your creation as we have seen millions of fishes wash up on shores; thousands of whales; millions of birds; thousands and millions of cattle die. They have died, and we call out to You Oh God for Your mercy. We pray and petition for Your creation, Oh God, that You will hear our prayers for You have provided sustenance for us through Your creation.

We can enjoy the food from the ocean; we can enjoy the splendor of Your hands and food for our human survival. We cannot exist, Oh God without

Your sustaining power. We beg You, Oh Most High, all-powerful God that You will have mercy upon Your creation, we stand in the gap. Oh Father God, if we ignore Your creation and do not intervene and cry out unto You Lord God, who will cry out for Your handiwork. We pray, dear God, we are hopeful, and we believe. We are asking You for Your mercy. Wherever there is destruction from man, let our law enforcement be cognizant of the issues that are at hand. Let us promptly respond, so we may save what we are destroying. Oh God, You alone, sustain our existence, not just our existence as humans, but the animals also. We depend on Your creation; You have given Your creation for our survival. Lord, as the work of your hands, give us the grace and the hearts to care for your creation that Your Name may be exalted. We trust You, and we believe You; we honor You Oh, most High God. We thank You so much; we have so much to be thankful for, You are an eternal God. You are all we will ever need. You are everything, Amen.

12. Prayer for Favor in the Earth, in the Air and in the Water

You are Oh God, the living water. When I am thirsty, I come to You Oh Majestic and Awesome God. You fill me to the brim until my cup is full and running over. Your grace has kept us. You provide the rain; You hold back the oceans. Your peace is upon the rivers. You allow us to drink from the wells of healthy streams of water. Most High and Awesome God, we petition You for towns and cities throughout this nation. You will heal the water, and You will restore the sea. Any devastation that's causing damage to the oceans and killing the entire ocean life, we pray for Your mercy, Oh Lord God Almighty. Where the water is tainted, and the pipes are old throughout this nation from which we drink, God, we pray that You will give our leaders grace and compassion and wisdom to make the drinking water safe. You are the creator of all things on the earth, the water in the oceans, mountains, trees, and animals; they all work in harmony at Your command. Oh God. We cannot make it without You, God. We do not even want to think about trying to make it without You, God. If we decide to exist without You, God: we are nothing. We could never be anything without You, God. We would never exist without Your grace upon us and upon this earth. We petition You, Most Holy and awesome God. Have mercy upon us and the planet-earth-that You have given us to manage; that You will pour out blessed water that we may enjoy. Your awesomeness and Your greatness that Your animals, Your sea life, the birds, and all creeping things upon the earth will rejoice in You because of Your magnanimity. Let Your light shine upon us, Oh merciful God, and we will forever sing praise unto Your Name in jubilation and adoration for You are the only true God, Amen.

13. Prayer for Our Neighborhoods

God, You have blessed us with culture, languages, and many different groups of people upon this earth. You love us so much that You give us communities; You give us friends; You give us the joy to be together with our friends and neighbors. We thank You, Heavenly Father, for Your gift of other people with whom we can interact in the community. We thank You for all the beautiful neighborhoods, architecture, landscaping, and characteristics You have given us in the various areas. Dear God in heaven, look upon the neighbors and the neighborhoods that are struggling with violence, crime, and poverty; lift them. We pray, let there be wisdom, let there be a desire for peace upon every neighborhood experiencing disturbance, gang activity, drug and alcohol abuse, prostitution, or any element of crime in these neighborhoods. We pray for peace; we pray for Your deliverance; we pray that You will give our law enforcement the grace to work with these communities in peace. God, we pray for respect by the law enforcement, and in return, by the people in all of our communities that there will be peace; there will be hope; there will be prosperity and Your blessings. God, You said, "We have not because we ask not," and we trust and believe that You will bless our many neighborhoods in our community, in our state, in our nation. God, we lift You high, we worship You, we honor You, we say glory onto Your Name. We declare victory belongs to You Oh God. Victory only comes from Your peace, tranquility, and salvation. We thank You Oh God, we thank You, we believe, and we receive for these neighborhoods by faith that You will bless each neighborhood across this nation in Jesus' Name, Amen.

14. Prayer for Peace in the Parks and Recreational Areas

Master and Savior, Lord of all the earth, all that exists, glory and honor to Your Name. You created the world, the earth, and all that is in it. You have given man the stewardship to manage Your creation. Thank You for the land that we are able to enjoy in so many ways. God, thank You that we can benefit mentally, emotionally, and spiritually from just looking at nature. Looking at Your wondrous creation, all that You have done, Oh God, our parks and recreational areas throughout this community and this land, state and nation. God, we pray for Your hands to be upon these areas. Protect the people who go to enjoy those areas. God, we pray for the workers who take care of these areas within our communities and our nation. God give, Your servants, grace. Oh Lord God, these places were designed by man for the enjoyment of people to play, not for unlawful activities. Bless these parks and recreational areas that they would be safe. As the families have picnics, are hiking, or just the children playing in the play areas, God let there be safety. Give the managers an understanding of what kind of chemicals they should use in maintenance, substances that would be eco-friendly and won't cause harm to anyone's health. Bless the parks and recreational areas to be full of joy and peace, and an overwhelming portion of Your grace, as families and individuals enjoy these areas that You've given us to manage and enjoy. We say, "Great is Thy faithfulness, Morning by morning, new mercy's I see all You have given, Your grace has provided, Great is Thy faithfulness, Great is Thy faithfulness," Oh Lord Amen.

15. Prayer for Direction During Finance

God, I am honored that You have allowed me an opportunity to come before You in Your presence. I thank You, Oh, King of Kings and Lord of Lords. You are all and everything to the whole universe. You are the great I AM. You are benevolent; You are glorious; You are victorious; thank You so much, Father. I bring my petition before You. You said that You were not the author of confusion. God, I pray that You will give direction in my life, and my family members lives God. Please let them know what type of jobs to get, what studies to do if in school, what kind of degree or whether they should go back to school. What type of work they should be doing; should it be the ministry? Help us, Lord. God, I pray for my family, myself, my finances, God, open the doors so that our needs will be taken care of, even to the degree that we are able to help other people take care of their needs. May we take care of the needs of the widows, the poor, and those who are less fortunate God. I ask for Your blessings upon our children and all of my family members. God, I pray that You, through me, will show Your glory, and I will be a blessing to Your name, in the name of Jesus, Amen.

16. Prayer for Vitality of Health

God, You are the Savior of the world. You are the air which we breathe; the water that we drink; the food that we eat. Oh God, You know everything about us. You understand our going and coming. You understand our illnesses. You understand our body type. You understand the type of food that we need for the body. Lord, hear our prayers. Guide us to the right sustenance for our bodies. Keep us in the right frame of mind to listen to what You are saying. Show us through our bodies what to eat, and know the right foods for our bodies according to Your will and plan for good health. God gives us a high level of sensitivity and obedience to keep Your order, so we can see our lives blessed; therefore, our health can function in order. God, I thank You for prayer, and I trust in Your holy name and

Your Holy word. I give You glory; I give You honor, and I give you praise. I ask for Your blessings upon my family in Jesus' name, Amen.

17. Prayer for Salvation

Oh God, You are delightful; You are miraculous; You are beautiful; more beautiful than the ocean and all that's in it. God, we thank You; we need You, and we call upon Your name. Salvation and blessings, we pray upon our relatives and our friends. Lord, we ask You to reveal Yourself to them, and they will submit to Your calling, Oh God. We know as we all submit to You; we will spend eternity with You. We desire to see our relatives spend eternity with You and with us as the greater family. God, we love You. Lord bless our prayers; strengthen our relatives; draw them unto Yourself in Jesus' Name, Amen.

18. Prayer for Intimate Relationship with God

Oh God in heaven, great are Your mighty works; great are Your hands upon the earth; great are Your hands in our lives Father. God, I pray for Your peace, for Your unity, for Your prosperity upon my family members. Your grace will rest upon all marriages, upon their children, upon their lives, their health, and every aspect Father. Grant them Your peace, Your unity, and Your love. We know You are the Giver of good gifts Lord; we petition You for a good gift to bond our relationships in Jesus' name, Amen.

19. Prayer against Addiction

Dear God of Mercy and God of Grace, we thank You and praise You. We glory in Your name. We thank You for Your power to heal; to deliver; to make whole; Father, we thank You. Your hands are the most powerful entity of our dependence. We thank You. You have solved many problems in the past. We come to You right now, Lord, for those who are struggling with many addictions. We pray You will help those who are having issues with alcohol or any type of substance abuse. We pray, Oh God, that You will bring deliverance; You will bring healing and restoration. God, You said, "If we asked it would be given, and we have not because we asked not." Father God, we ask You for Your mercy and Your deliverance. We thank You for Your mighty hand, and we believe it is done in Jesus' Name, Amen.

20. Prayer for Absolute Peace

God, You are so glorious; You are victorious in all of Your ways. I honor You, and I give You praise; I glorify You; I give You my life Father. There are many things taking place all over the world. Even in my life, some disturbances occur occasionally and sometimes often. You, Oh Lord, have the power to give me peace beyond all understanding. Give me peace that no one else can offer. God let Your rest be upon me, Lord, Amen

21. Prayer for Heavenly Provision

Oh God, I cry out to You because You are so great. You are the awesome power of all the Earth. Thank you. You are there for us in every way. Lord, in Your word, You said we have not because we ask not. You also said if we delight ourselves in You, You will give us the desires of our hearts. Oh God, as I come to You in need, You know much better Than I Know. You stated in Your word that You are willing to meet our needs according to Your riches and Glory in Christ Jesus. Father, I pray for the resources that I need to take care of my concerns. I bring it to You. Oh God in Heaven because You are the Creator of the Universe. You alone can meet every need that I have; thank you, Oh God for Your word; thank You Oh God, for taking care of all of my needs in Jesus' Name, Amen

22. Prayer for Divine Direction

Thank You, Father, in Heaven for You control everything: the birds of the air; the fish of the sea; You are the God of the whole creation. Lord, many roads lead to many different directions, but You stated in Your word that You are not the author of confusion. I pray, Oh Lord right now for Your direction; for Your guidance; for Your love to empower me to do Your will. Guide me, Oh God, this day; guide me, Oh God, in the direction that I seek from You. You are the Author of life and You direct all of Your creation, Oh God Almighty, direct my path.

23. Prayer for Faith in God

Oh Lord How Majestic is Your Name in all the Earth. I give You honor glory and praise. Thank You, Father, for the issues that I'm faced with each day. Lord, in Your word, You stated that faith without works is dead. Also, You said that faith is the substance of things hoped for and the evidence of things not seen. I thank You, Oh Lord. You also said that if I had enough faith as a grain of a mustard seed, we could speak to the mountains, "Be thou removed," it would happen. Father in the Name of Jesus, I pray that You will give me strength; You will give me Faith; You will grant me the courage to believe You for faith. Give me strength this day to trust and have faith in Jesus' Name, Amen

24. Prayer for Strength in the Lord

Dear God in heaven, thank You for this wonderful day. We are glorified through You, and we give You honor. We also praise and thank you for allowing us to be in this great nation, thank you for everything. Lord, I pray You will give me the strength to go through this day to do the things You would have me to do. Bring glory to Your Name, let my heart be in the place that You want it to be. Let my feet walk in the steps that You want them to walk. Bring the people, which You would have me minister to, today and share Your love as you see fit. Give me Your strength in my health, mentally, physically, and every way that I may serve You better, in Jesus' Name, Amen.

25. Prayer for Our Institutions

Oh God, my soul cries out to Your greatness. My life is Yours, Oh God. My mind is in Your hands, my Father. God, I pray for our institutions; our universities and schools Lord, You said, "People perish for the lack of knowledge." God open the minds of our young people, middle-aged people, and our older people. Give them a learning and a teachable spirit. Open their hearts to learning, Father. I pray You will bring upon this group of institutions; universities, schools, and places of learning proper teaching. I pray that teaching will inspire; teaching will proclaim the truth about health, life, and every area of learning.

26. Prayer for Our Industries

Victory Oh God, victory Oh God is Yours forever. You are the King; You are the Creator; You are the Almighty. You will live forever and ever and ever, Father God. Thank You for our industries; thank You for the businesses all over the cities, the states, and this nation, God. I pray for the industries Lord God. I pray for innovation and creativity that they will continue to prosper; that they will continue to be a source of provision for the people in the towns and states across this land. God, I pray You will raise Your people with creative and innovative ideas. Give them hearts to use their resources to further Your gospel. Bring hope, life, and salvation to the world. God, only You can move mountains; only You, Oh God can strengthen hearts; only You, Oh God, can give ideas and fresh ideas that will result in great benefits to people on this earth. It is You, Oh God, who controls all things. We pray for Your influence and for Your blessings to be upon our industries, in Jesus' Name, Amen

27. Prayer for Our Governors and Mayors in the Helm of Affairs

Oh Lord God, You are my hope; You are my salvation; You are the answer to every prayer. Lord, I bring before You, the governors, leaders, and the mayors of each state. God, I pray You will give them wisdom; You will give them grace; You will give them peace and the proper insights to interact with our federal government. Lord, I pray for Your wisdom to be with them in the judicial system. Give them the wisdom to judge righteously and to choose in a Godly manner. Father, I pray You will bring prosperity and blessings upon each of our cities of each state. God, give our mayor favor with the governor and that the governor's relationship will be blessed as he collaborates with all the mayors of the states. God, we thank You, we ask You for Your blessings upon their families and every aspect of their lives. God give them Your grace and tenderness to hear Your voice and to abide by Your word. We ask all of these things in Jesus' Name, Amen

28. Prayer for Our States and Cities

Our Country is Yours, Oh God of heaven and earth. You are victorious in all of Your ways; there is none like You. You are like the flowers and the blooms of spring. We thank You for allowing our prayers to go up to heaven, God, our cities and states all over this nation are in need of Your power; Your presence; Your comfort God. Where there is crime, bring salvation, where there is death and destruction, bring peace Father. Where there is homelessness and poor living on the streets-give Your people, the body of Christ, the heart of Mercy. God, I pray for those who are in hardships in any way, in the towns, cities across this nation give the mayors and the governors wisdom and compassion to know how to address these issues. God, give the governors and the mayors of the cities, the hearts to run after You, God. Lord help us to be holy that we will have prayers that are effective onto Your throne, God Almighty in the Name of Jesus hear our prayers in Jesus' Name, Amen

29. Prayer for Our Nation's Leaders

Lord, You created the moon, the sun, the stars, and the heavens, Oh God. You created the earth and all that is in it. You control governments; presidents and You are in control of all things, Oh God. Dear God, look upon our land, our president, upon his family; upon every branch of government, the senate, the congress, the mayors and governors, towns, cities, and states. We pray, Oh God, that You will speak to their hearts, that they will be open to listening to Your word and seek direction to know You Lord, for the sake of our nation, in Jesus' Name, Amen

30. Prayer for Money

Thank You, God, for Your resources You have given us. You have entrusted us with treasures. We need wisdom and understanding of how to use them. Thank you, most gracious and benevolent King of all the earth. You have provided for us in our time of need. Wonderful and magnificent, Lord of all creation, I pray to You for wisdom, understanding, a gift of Your knowledge on how to manage and utilize the gifts You give us.

Any resource that You have given, You have the power to direct me on how to use these blessings for good. I need You Oh God, to direct my path and give me a clear mind. Direct my vision to handle my finances so that I may take care of all of my needs. Lord give me associates that will be wise and with a good understanding of how to manage and use finances. Father give me the wisdom needed to know how to be a fine steward of that which you have given, especially to those who are in need. All that I do, Oh God, with the money and resources which You give to me, let it all be done as unto You. Let me use it selflessly and to your ultimate purpose. As a blessing unto Your Name, let me use it, so you may be glorified in me with all of the resources that You have gifted me. Allow me to understand the proper way and channels of how to obtain the money. Take away any reluctance, fear, or anguish about money. Help me to understand that all money belongs to You, and money is only a tool. Grant me the gift of how to use money wisely in Jesus' Name, Amen.

31. Prayer for Money and Wise Investments

God, I am forever grateful that You have made available many opportunities for investing and storing away for the future. You are interested in our ability to save resources through investments. Heavenly Father, without Your understanding, where would we be? For that reason, we cry out to You for Your understanding of where we should invest our money. Lord, should it be the stock market; real estate; currency; silver or gold? Please, Oh God, let me know and give me insight into where to invest the resources that You have given me. You are the Divine Creator of everything. What Direction should I go? You understand my ability to comprehend. Please, Oh God, let Your light shine upon me. Let me function under the enlightenment of Your Holy Spirit. Give me the insight to be a wise investor and a wise steward of my financial gifts. As I gather resources to invest for the future, even this Oh Lord God, let me do it as unto You so that You may be exalted in my life. Thank You again, dear God, for the resources that You have entrusted unto me. I pray, Oh God, that I will forever give You honor, thanksgiving, glory, and praise to Your mighty Name, in Jesus' Name, Amen.

Section Two

PERSONAL DEVELOPMENT

When I think about personal development, I think of the scripture in the book of James that says, "Faith without works is dead." What this means is that if you don't give anything or take action, you don't get anything. If you allow fate to take its course, you will be disappointed with whatever comes your way. Have you ever wondered or probably complained about why things went the way they did? Sometimes, while striving to meet some particular goals, we might be blocked by the hand of God if what we are pursuing is not in accordance with His will. For instance, we all know what happened to Paul on the road to Damascus; or when Balaam heard the donkey speak and when Jonah deviated from God's directive to go to Nineveh.

Activating God's blessings demands total compliance to His will on the road of achieving our personal development. Our compliance is the "work," while the act of waiting for the expected result is the "faith." To develop ourselves personally, knowing the changes to make is not enough, but what is important is how we will make those changes because these changes do not happen easily except in steadfast adherence to Christ. The book of 2 Timothy 3:16-17 has provided us the guidance we need for this self-improvement, stating that God's word is necessary for teaching the truth, rebuking error, correcting faults, and giving instructions for right living. This simply indicates our vital need for the scriptures to govern our life.

I have illustrated personal development in accordance with the book of James, but I also want you to understand that it is a process of molding individual abilities, skills, gifts to maximize the potential of God's calling or purpose upon your life. This is achievable, as I have said with the scriptures, and it should not surprise you to know that such a trait dwells in the holy book. This is why God is the one who initiated the plan for us to grow, develop, and improve with Christ Jesus. In 2 Corinthians 3:18, He set down the rules for you and me to reach a life of increasing glory. We must also understand that development in Christ focuses on the following things: understanding yourself in Christ Jesus, developing and training your spirit, soul, mind, and body in alignment with God's purpose. Living a life that conforms to God's design, plan and achieve faith goals, succumbing to the will of God and living while maximizing your potential in Christ Jesus. All these are centered on personal development with Christ (1 Corinthians 9:25).

Seeking Divine Mentorship

The act of mentorship is a relationship between a more experienced person and a less experienced individual. In this situation, the former guides the latter. When I think of mentorship, these scriptures; Hebrews 13:7, Joshua 1:1 and Matthew 4:18-22 (to mention a few) come to mind. In the verses I have listed, we see God's continuous mentorship and guidance in his servants. In the Old Testament, Israel was given Moses (Exodus 3: 8-10), Samuel the prophet needed Eli at some point in his life (Samuel 3: 1-16), and David, the man after God's heart, also needed Saul, (1 Samuel 18: 3-4). Today we know that we are in an era of grace through the introduction and the acceptance of Christ Jesus, but seeking divine wisdom from the soul the Lord has called, will help lead us through the bumpier harvest into our divine destination.

Lately, I have come to notice that at the beginning of every year, most of us tend to have new year resolutions, and in the long run, none of these resolutions are established. We always fall, a victim of this, because as true believers in Christ Jesus, developing oneself without Christ is like storing water in a basket. Thus these resolutions are proclaimed by our human name, desire, strength, benefit, and personal gain. They either fail or do not come to life because they are centered on you, I mean self, or your own strength. The book of 1 Timothy 3:5 also shows us that people will hold to the outward form of our religion, but reject its real power. This means that we can make plans for ourselves, but without the signature of Christ Jesus, which is the real power, those plans are as good as zero. There is no fruitfulness in fate taking its course if the faith in God is not established.

We must ask God for a new heart because without one, we would continue to fall in and out of life, and this is the reason why most people feel lost even before they reach the peak of their human life. They will hate themselves and blame others for their failures, and such persons will always look for excuses to praise themselves. All these are eliminated from the life of a true-believing Christian because the act of developing yourself in Christ is an exhilarating and liberating experience. The truth here is that resolutions, plans without Christ Jesus are barriers that deprived us of deepening our relationship with our Father in Heaven. We feel we are Christians, but in our hearts, we are aware of the distance between our Heavenly Father and our spirit.

I have revised 30 different topics focused on areas of our life that we can focus on to enhance our life's outcomes. From education, health, finances, and relationships to the environment. The reason for doing this is that I was frustrated with myself for not achieving the goals that I set out to achieve or for not being as organized as I wanted to be. I came up with these topics to look at ways that I could enhance my life. I pray with all sincerity that these topics will be a real benefit to you as you prayerfully focus on them, may your life be fulfilled. I have also provided a list of goal setting ideas so that you can write your goals down and continue to review them on a monthly, weekly, and daily basis.

The Role Of Personal Development In Your Life As A Christian

It is no doubt that you and I are meant to be progress-beings in Christ Jesus, ascending from one realm of glory to another. Using Matthew 16: 24-25, "Whoever wants to be my disciple must deny themselves and take up their cross and follow me. For whoever wants to save their life will lose it, but whoever loses their life for me will find it." This is what Jesus told us in his time on earth, implying that we must continuously be in denial of ourselves for the calling of Christ and His fullness to develop in us as Christians. If this is not done, then I want you to know that the whole process of personal development is incomplete, (Ecclesiastes 10:10, John 3:30; 12: 24-25).

I want us to look back at the creation and see what it clearly shows us. We are aware that everything living, whether it is an animal or plant, struggles to attain/reach its maximum potential. There is never a tree or shrub (healthy) that will choose to grow halfway and quit or an animal that will choose to remain a pup until it runs out of its lifespan. There is nothing like a lazy mango tree, lion, leopard, petunias, or even the minute ants. Every living thing created by God is designed and in tuned to succeed in its destiny, even if it has to fight every day to do so. There is no living thing that can be called the handwork of Satan; they are all a gift from God which He created—even bacteria have significant uses in our lives. We all can agree that the creation is not just a gift but a miracle in consecrating the power of our Heavenly Father.

Humanity on the other hand was granted "choice," and this has given us the ability to settle for less even when He created and crafted more for us. Looking at the life of Abraham in the Old Testament, we see that Abraham chose to follow God, and thus God made him the richest man, this can be likened as developing oneself in Christ Jesus. For us to develop ourselves correctly, we must follow God. David and Solomon are perfect examples of what it means to build personal development in God. David was anointed, and he always communed and worshipped the Father. Solomon could have requested for anything, but he chose wisdom, which as well came from God and what can we perceive from the bible? In their time, Israel was at its peak. It was the richest, strongest, and most powerful nation because God had built this himself right from the departure of Egypt. If we do not push God out of our lives, we will continue to grow in the spirit.

Even today, in the earlier era, when America embraced Christianity, our country snowballed above other nations, accomplishing and making history, the land became richer, the standard of living was higher. Our children were more astute than others. But now, we are gradually taking Him out by abandoning His principles, and we all can see the repercussions of that decision, instead of looking to Him as our source of blessings, refuge, anchor, and guide. We now set our hopes on the government, the rich, or ourselves when neither possesses the power to help us grow spiritually. This decision has allowed the enemy to counterfeit biblical instructions to his false glory. Still, Christians who strive to recognize and adhere to God's original principles will manifest blessings that bring glory and honor to our Heavenly Father, who is indeed the author of our faith.

Using Jesus As Our Model For Personal Development

I have outlined this in the simplest form, so that we all may understand.

Divine awareness

- His name Jesus means, "The one who will save people from sin"; Luke 2:22.

- Luke 2: 29-35, Simeon prophesied that He would be known as the Savior and will be a Light to the world.
- His birth was marveled, and His parents dedicated Him to God upon His coming to earth; Luke 2:33; 2:22-24.
- When Jesus was thirty years, He enunciated his life mission; Luke 4:17-21.
- He traveled from one place to another abandoning self, because He knew the need to spread the gospel; Luke 4:42-43.

Divine life

- As a child Jesus partook in all religious festivals with His family; Luke 2:41.
- When He was twelve years old, He visited His Father's house and took delight in sharing the word of God with religious leaders.
- In His young age he worked as a carpenter; Mark 6:2-3, Luke 4:22.
- He continually practiced self-abandonment—we were told he prayed, fasted in the wilderness alone and also overcame temptation; Matthew 4:1-11.
- Jesus never followed the decision of the crowds, especially when they demanded his presence (this proves he was not of the world); instead, he prayed in lonely places; Luke 5:16.
- In Gethsemane, he overcame his emotions and submitted totally to the will of the Father; Luke 22:39-44, John 18:11.

Divine generosity and grace

- He was baptized at thirty by John cleansing Himself from sin and was gracefully blessed by the Father, which was done as an example to us; Luke 2: 21-22.

- Jesus grew in strength and wisdom because we are told of the heavenly words and parables that left His lips; Matthew 13:1-50, Luke 2:40-52; 4:22.
- When He began His ministry, He healed, delivered, taught, and trained people in the ways of God without earthly gain; Luke 4: 31.

Divine power

- Jesus never relied on His power but the power of God; Luke 5:17.
- Before choosing the apostles, He seeks God; Luke 6:12-13.
- He was so filled with the power of God that he could calm the storm, walk on water. And his clothes radiated this power; Luke 8:22-25; 8:42-48.
- With the power of God, He cast and vanquished demons.

Divine educator

- He initiated the act of discipleship and was known among true believers as Rabboni (teacher); Matthew 4:18-20, John 20:16.
- Jesus kept the company with like-minds; Luke 22:15.

Divine self

- When He transfigured on the mountain top, His body radiated the glory and light of God; Mark 9:2-8, Luke 9:28-36.
- He encompasses boundless love; thus, He suffered and died on the cross to bring us back to God, Mark 15: 1-37, Luke 23:26-47.
- Through the power of God, he resurrected from the dead, proving to us that He conquered sin, death, and hell.
- Jesus ascends into Heaven and sends us the Holy Spirit for guidance; Luke 24:50-53.

I believe with all my heart that God wants us to accomplish great and mighty things. I think of the song that Billy Preston sang, "Nothing from nothing leaves nothing," and that is true, if you give a lot, you'll get a lot in return. Even in the scripture, it says in one passage, "Give and it shall be given unto you, good measure pressed down and shaken together and running over, shall men give into your bosom. For with the same measure that you give, it shall be measured to you."

Rhythm and Patterns to Personal Development

Knowledge and understanding are the key ingredients to achieving success and attaining our personal development. Without either, our potentials can never be fully maximized. To develop certain patterns (Isaiah 29:16; 64:8), the starting point is to understand God's unique patterns of development and what he expects you to metamorphose into – Exodus 25:40. In other words, personal development in the life of a true believer is not one to be filled with trials and errors or simply a mere blind pursuit. Because we are told from the bible that our Heavenly Father is the potter and we, His children, are the clay. Originally, a potter works with different shapes of molds that are unknown to the clay, and the clay cannot decide its fate.

Therefore we must learn to trust God even when we are physically blind. Our sight by His power should remain unwavering because if we have accepted to be His clay (children of God), then we can never know our mold because the Lord is still working on us. All that is needed is to seek God's face and just believe that He has greater things in store for us; Jeremiah 29:11 says, "For I know the plans I have for you, declares the Lord, plans to prosper you and not to harm you, plans to give you hope and a future."

Utilizing the rhythm of every season is rhythm as well as it is a pattern, trials and difficulties arise in one way or the other, but as Christians, we must add value to such situations, (Daniel 1:1-17). In the book of Esther,

(1:10-20; 2:15-20), it shows how Esther, a humble woman, was made queen over other maidens who adorned themselves with things of the world. God's creation can plan, but God takes the final say, and this goes further to emphasize the need of God in developing oneself.

It also teaches us that no matter how sordid our plans are, without the invitation of God in them, it is futile. Sometimes we are faced with habits and behaviors that hold us back both spiritually and physically. We would say to ourselves:

"I will stop this,"
"This is the last,"
"I will do this,"
"I will put an end to this addiction."

But after a short while the habit arises, why do you think this is so? Why do these habits/addictions keep occurring from time to time? It is because the author of the story has been excluded. As we are clay, so we are books. God needs to be the one to write how we improve ourselves spiritually, physically, mentally, financially, socially, educationally, and in every other aspect that entails living as true believers. You cannot be the author of your life, and if you begin this in the morning before noon, all that was achieved will crumble, but those who build and develop themselves upon the solid rock (Christ Jesus) will never know such events. They become disciples after the resurrection, filled with the spirit and achievements become ceaseless.

Going back to rhythms of seasons, Daniel also did not backslide during captivity; instead, he added value to his life, and the Lord showed his power. Joseph was sold into slavery by his brothers, but still, he remained in God. He continued to build himself in Jehovah, and in the end, he brought glory unto his God and his tribe. Also, the recession we see in our time is the same as these captivities I have mentioned, but rather than allowing it to under develop our Christian faith, we must add value to it, thus, improving our spiritual growth in Christ Jesus.

This booklet suggests that there are thirty practical concepts that can activate God's blessings in our lives; we know this because we have read in the Bible, "Faith without work is death." This 30 days practical concept is filled with daily working activities that can help you attain your personal development as you pursue faith that can activate God's blessings for your life.

There are rhythms and patterns in all living things. Discover yours, work with them, and make them work for you. Your rhythms and patterns to attaining personal development are like a roadmap and fuel, directing you and helping you to arrive at your destination in life. Kindly endeavor to read this section of the book thoroughly in one uninterrupted sitting, integrate the concepts, and pray for that transformation you've been longing for. Look through the exercises to decide if you need to utilize any of them.

It is recommended that you walk for at least twenty minutes each day. Then, each morning when you're awake, read one concept, familiarize yourself with the daily scriptural readings, and integrate that day's principle as your daily guide for the day. Think about the concept, then rise, shine and do the exercise you may have decided to do. Be sure to walk or exercise twenty minutes during the day: Before work, during your lunch break or after work — whatever time fits your schedule. Then, when you retire that night, go over the concept again. Sleep on it. The next day, go on to the next concept in the list and follow the routine, do the exercise if necessary. One new concept a day will bring you to all thirty concepts by the end of the month, and you will be exercising regularly, as well. Then start at the beginning again. Follow through, day by day, month by month. Then, stand back and assess your success after a full 12 months. You will be amazed and gratified at what you have achieved, and how much better your life has become.

The 30 days Daily Rhythm Activities Toward Your Personal Development

DAY 1: VISUALIZE WHO YOU WANT TO BE

Whatever you can imagine clearly, you can cause to happen. Whoever you want to be, you can become. Create yourself the way you want to be because God sees you the way He created you. He wants you to activate His blessings by being the real you–the person you are or want to become in every aspect of life, including character, in integrity, spiritually, creatively, career-wise, financially, appearance, in the eyes of your loved ones, your colleagues, the community. Think about it. If you could be the person you want to become, picture yourself in an exact way, doing the things that would be compatible with that picture. Visualize yourself doing what you want most to do as far as your life work is concerned. Visualize yourself, your appearance, your non-judgmental and helpful attitude toward others, your ability to love and provide for those closest to you, your helpfulness and standing in your community, your spirituality, morality, ethics, and compassion in every phase and level of your life.

Scriptural Reading for the day:

Deuteronomy 5:33 – "Walk in obedience to all that the LORD your God has commanded you, so that you may live and prosper and prolong your days in the land that you will possess."

DAY 2: SET GOALS

Now that you have visualized the person you want to be; just how God himself sees you, you must now set goals to achieve that end. Do not look at this step as overwhelming, but as a joyous opportunity that will lead you to activating God's blessings for your life: Remember, anything you can imagine, you can achieve. Yesterday, you learned how to visualize yourself as the person you want to become, did some ideas come to you about how you could achieve your dream? The more you think about the person you want to become, the more plans begin to develop in your mind. Think creatively. Of all the steps, you need to arrive at your goal, which should come first? Which can be done simultaneously with others? Which can be put off, while you work on the beginning steps? How long will it take you to arrive at your goal? Think about it clearly and creatively. Above all, think about it positively, with enthusiasm and with joy.

Scriptural Reading for the day:

Jeremiah 29:11 – "I know the plans I have for you," declares the Lord, "plans to prosper you and not to harm you, plans to give you hope and a future."

DAY 3: CREATE A CREATIVE ENVIRONMENT

Design an area in your home — be it in a house, an apartment, or one room — a place with a comfortable chair, a desk, or a table on which to write, and a good light. Buy a notebook, laptop or smart phone that you will use for this project and this alone. Be sure to have sharpened pencils or a pen that flows well. In short, a place that is conducive to comfort, a place where God's blessings can be activated. Be free from distractions, and create a place that you will look forward to going as you plan your goals. This will act as your command center. A cork bulletin board will also be helpful near your special place — preferably in the back of your desk or table where you can glance up at it as you are thinking or writing.

You can tack up photographs from magazines of the people you admire most, photographs of your family and best friends. These are the people who wish you well and who will be supportive of your efforts. An attractive green plant can create a feeling of renewal and rejuvenation. Certain colors in the room can convey feelings of peace, can stimulate creativity, can elevate your mood. Keep this desk area free from clutter. Clutter hinders creative thinking.

Scriptural Reading for the day:

Proverbs 21:5 "The plans of the diligent leads to profit as surely as haste leads to poverty."

DAY 4: CREATE A PLAN AND WRITE IT DOWN

Now that you have a workable command center, proceed to open your laptop, smart phone or notebook and pick up that pencil or pen. On day one, you've learned how to visualize who you want to be because God wants you to be blessed, and He wants you to achieve more. On day two, you thought about how to go about achieving those goals. Now it's time to write down these thoughts. When you can see your thoughts and goals in writing, then you're on another level of self-discovery. You can refer back to them whenever you want to refresh your memory and keep your plan alive. Now is the time to create your master plan. Write down your thoughts as they come. Then go over them and rearrange them in a logical and workable order. You will see how easily your plan unfolds if you can clearly think about it. By doing this important step, you will see how organization in your life is like the roadmap we spoke of in the introduction. Again, attack this joyously. Is there any better feeling than becoming a master of your fate, of being in charge of your life?

Scriptural Reading for the day:

Psalms 37:5 – "Commit your way to the LORD; trust in him and he will do this."

DAY 5: FIND YOUR RHYTHMS AND PATTERNS

We all have rhythms in our life. The rhythms in any 24-hour period are called circadian rhythms and affect most living creatures. Some of us are morning people — we arise without effort and face the day with a clear head and energy because God allowed us. Others are night people: We are most creative and can accomplish more in the nighttime than in the day. By now, you should be aware of your rhythms: You may be full of pep at your workplace at 11 in the morning, sleepy after lunch, regain your energy around 3, start to slow down again after 5:30. Or you may have an entirely different rhythm. If you haven't paid attention to these natural time slots, begin to do so now. Keep a diary on your smart phone or a ruled sheet of paper will do. Jot down your peak hours, your low times. In this way, you will become conscious of the hours when you can be most creative and energetic. This is when you can attack a problem or a plan and accomplish a great deal. God has given us a wealth of knowledge to tap from; tap into this knowledge to further strengthen your goals. If goals and organization are used as your roadmap, your fuel is utilizing your peak times. By being aware of and using your roadmap and fueling yourself with your natural rhythms, your destination will be easier to reach.

Scriptural Reading for the day:

Isaiah 28:13 – "So then, the word of the LORD to them will become: Do this, do that, a rule for this, a rule for that; a little here, a little there."

DAY 6: GET AN ATTITUDE — A POSITIVE ONE

A positive attitude is necessary for achieving success. Notice how you respond to suggestions, new ideas, and comments. If you immediately respond with a negative comment, find immediate fault or flaws, you're probably shooting down the possibilities of entering a new adventure, a new way of life, a fun opportunity, making new friends, or creating a good impression. Think about it: Negatives don't breed positives. Try to develop the habit of first responding positively to whatever is presented to you (unless it's unlawful, wrong, will harm yourself or others). Try to see the good in things. That doesn't mean you have to accept what is proposed or offered. It just puts you in the right frame of mind to properly analyze it. You may decide to reject it — but for the right reasons, without the cloud of negativity, putting a dark spin on it. If you practice having a positive attitude, it may seem fake to you at first but it's not. Developing and nurturing a positive attitude can become customary too. And it will bring positive things to you. Remember, negativity repels; positiveness attracts. A negative mind is a mind that distrust God, and He really dislikes a shaky faith that cannot move a mountain. Be a positive thinker.

Scriptural Reading for the day:

Philippians 4:8 – "Finally, brothers and sisters, whatever is true, whatever is noble, whatever is right, whatever is pure, whatever is lovely, whatever is admirable--if anything is excellent or praiseworthy--think about such things."

DAY 7: BUILD FAITH AND COMMITMENT

Distrust and jealousy destroy our faith, and God's commitment to activate God's blessings for our lives. When you know in your heart that those you love also loves you, then, you are practically building your faith and commitment towards God and others. This may seem simplistic, but it is the basis for all love and trust among people, and without it, it is impossible to go forward positively. Your commitment to your family, friends, employer, co-workers will be rewarded positively. Yes, sometimes we misplace our trust in those who are adept at deception, but why should you become mistrusting and cynical, skeptical, and unloving because a few people have acted poorly? Rise above them. Take the high road. Wouldn't you rather do that than mistrust a good person or be wrongfully jealous of a sincere relationship? Build faith. Strengthen your commitments.

Scriptural Reading for the day:

Mark 11:24 – "Therefore I tell you, whatever you ask for in prayer, believe that you have received it, and it will be yours."

DAY 8: KNOWING YOU CAN CHANGE BRINGS FREEDOM

God has given us the power to change and grow. Spiritual and intellectual growth begin in the workplace, in your friendships and family relations. Stagnation, not allowing growth, is not natural or godly to our condition. Plants, trees, and flowers grow when properly tended. They become stunted, wither, and die without proper attention and even affection. Think back on the changes that have taken place in your life. If good, what brought them about? Were you open to change? Did you summon the courage to change? Did you help bring about the circumstances that led to the change? If the changes were not good, why was that? Were you not open to change? Were you not courageous enough to make a change? Did you close doors just before they were about to be opened? Permit yourself to change, when change is good. Allow your life to become gold. Allowing good changes in your life will give you a sense of freedom — a sense of moving ahead.

Scriptural Reading for the day:

Hosea 6:1 – "Come, let us return to the LORD. He has torn us to pieces but he will heal us; he has injured us but he will bind up our wounds."

DAY 9: BANISH FEAR BY BEING IN THE PRESENT

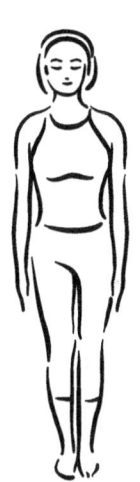

Fear is one of our greatest enemies. It cripples and flattens our faith if we are not truly rooted in the word of God. Being mindful of what you are doing every minute in the day is of great importance. Concentrate on the task at hand – your conversation with another and what they try to convey to you. Even when reading a book, give it your full concentration. This is what we mean when we suggest you be in the present. If you practice focusing, you may find that your mind wanders at first, but with conscious practice, you will always be in the present; at the moment be mindful of what you are doing. Fear has no way of entering a mind that is appropriately focused. If you can banish fear from your life, you will move forward in your life plan without hesitation, with joy and enthusiasm. Fear can hold you back from making bold, wise moves.

Scriptural Reading for the day:

Joshua 1:9 – "….be strong and courageous. Do not be afraid; do not be discouraged, for the LORD your God will be with you wherever you go."

DAY 10: KNOW THAT AN UNSEEN POWER IS THERE TO HELP YOU

I know you have experienced in your life that when one door closes on you — a door that you hoped fervently would open and lead you to a better life that another opens; instead, that leads you to an even better path than you had hoped for. Have you ever had the feeling that invisible hands are helping you when you most need them? This "unseen power" comes from the supreme God, and He is the one that gives energy to your inner strength and the hopes to manifest these attributes in your life. Whatever may be your faith, know that God is there to provide you with this power and that you must put in words — even if the words are said silently to yourself — exactly what it is you want to achieve. You may call this prayer; you may call it manifesting your needs; whichever it is, it should be stated clearly FOR YOUR EDIFICATION exactly and precisely what is needed in order to activate the hidden power.

Scriptural Reading for the day:

Joshua 1:9 – "….be strong and courageous. Do not be afraid; do not be discouraged, for the LORD your God will be with you wherever you go."

DAY 11: LOVE AND LIVE LIFE — GIVE A SMILE AWAY

God is love, and He wants us to live our lives in love and happiness. He wants us to radiate this love by smiling and being cheerful to others, and this is one of the easiest exercises you will ever do: As soon as you give a smile away, you will have it returned to you. When you smile in greeting, you make the recipient feel special and welcomed. Barriers often break down at the "onslaught" of a smile. When you smile, you can't feel sad. Try it. Think of something or someone pleasant and smile right now. When a friend or acquaintance calls you on the phone, say that person's name exultantly ("Bill!" "Mom!" "Janet!"). Make the person know he or she is special to you, and that you are thrilled and honored they have called you. Again, this may seem false at first but, as you grow  into this friendly way of being, you will begin to like people more, and your greetings and smiles will be 100 percent sincere. Don't be discouraged by grouches. No one ever permitted them to smile.

Scriptural Reading for the day:

1 John 4:7 – "Dear friends, let us love one another, for love comes from God. Everyone who loves has been born of God and knows God."

DAY 12: PRACTICE LISTENING AS YOU WOULD PRACTICE A SPORT

One of the greatest weapons we have as a child of God is the act of listening attentively to His words, and if we cannot cultivate this habit, we sure cannot activate His blessings in our lives. No one can play a sport perfectly at first – it takes practice. If we fail to listen to the person talking to us, how can we learn to listen to God when He speaks? Listening requires concentration, caring, proper responses, an appropriate facial expression, and body stance. Folding your arms across your chest when someone is talking to you forms an unspoken barrier. Be open. If seated, lean forward towards the speaker, demonstrating silently with this gesture your willingness to listen, to really hear what the person is telling you. From time to time, during a pause, summarize what that person has just told you in a few words, saying them to the speaker. Be mindful of practicing this technique during conversations throughout the day. Notice how your attentiveness is received by the speaker. You will gain by this daily practice, and your companion will acknowledge you silently as a valued listener.

Scriptural Reading for the day:

Col 4:6 – "Let your conversation be always full of grace, seasoned with salt, so that you may know how to answer everyone."

DAY 13: WHAT YOU GIVE IN A RELATIONSHIP YOU WILL RECEIVE

When we relate with God, we form a bond of father-to-children relationship. Thus, God directs, and we follow Him. This same principle applies to how we relate with our fellow human beings. Think about how you like to be treated: With courtesy, with attention, with admiration, with affection, with consideration, with compassion, with respect, with caring, with understanding. If you like to be treated well, you can be assured others do too. In these days, when rage seems to be triggered by the smallest provocation, think what a pleasant response can do. Try to understand the other person's viewpoint. Listen to it. Try to leave judgments to God. You know what is right for you, but perhaps it isn't right for another person — unless we're talking about absolutes, like good and evil, confront difficult situations: Talk things out calmly; listen to the other person's viewpoint. Always leave room for compromise. In a marriage, compatibility is almost always based on give and take, small compromises on both persons' part. Never take a relationship for granted: Work at it constantly, with love in your heart.

Scriptural Reading for the day:

Proverbs 11:25 – "A generous person will prosper; whoever refreshes others will be refreshed."

DAY 14: SHARE YOUR IDEAS WITH SUPPORTIVE PEOPLE

God's desire for us is to be successful, and that is why He created us both male and female. He already knows we need each other for growth and development. He wants us to support each other, love each other, and grow in knowledge; so that we can apply this principle to activate His blessings. So, when you share your ideas with supportive people, you will learn and grow. For instance, if you have a good idea about a new business, a new destination for your vacation, about trying a new hairstyle or clothing fashion, about sending your children to a private school, about trying a new restaurant; share it with others. Small changes or gigantic changes in your life can be shared with a really good, supportive friend, a friend you can trust to listen to your ideas without being instantly judgmental; a friend who will hear you out while you voice your thoughts — even change your thoughts while you're talking. A good friend will ask questions, which may stimulate deeper thinking, perhaps suggest alternative ideas. Whatever you decide to do, even though it may be to drop the new idea, you will have the comfort of knowing that a good friend has been through your thought process with you and perhaps may have added new dimensions to your thinking.

Scriptural Reading for the day:

Deuteronomy 28:12-13 – "¹²The LORD will open for you His good storehouse, the heavens, to give rain to your land in its season and to bless all the work of your hand; and you shall lend to many nations, but you shall not borrow. ¹³"The LORD will make you the head and not the tail, and you only will be above, and you will not be underneath, if you listen to the commandments of the LORD your God, which I charge you today, to observe *them* carefully,."

DAY 15: FIND A TRUE MENTOR

We all have someone God has placed in our lives for mentorship and guidance. This can be anybody, and the sole aim of this mentor is to direct our paths towards activating God's blessings for our lives. Reaching your goals is faster and more painless if you have a mentor to guide you through the maze of life. Persons you admire most are natural mentors for you: The reason you admire them is that they have achieved what you aspired. Hitch your wagon to their star. Ask for advice. Listen to their advice. Follow their advice if it matches your own set of moral, ethical, and spiritual standards. If it doesn't match, perhaps you need a different mentor. Let your mentor know how much you appreciate his or her interest in you. Make your mentor proud of you.

Scriptural Reading for the day:

John 10:27-28 – "My sheep listen to my voice; I know them, and they follow me. I give them eternal life, and they shall never perish; no one can snatch them out of My hand."

DAY 16: TAKE A GOOD LOOK AT YOURSELF

We are created in God's image, and if you observe yourself as if you're looking at a stranger. Are you pleased with what you see? Do you look like someone created in God's image? Is your grooming excellent? Do your appearances reflect who God wants you to be? Your hairstyle? The way you carry yourself, does it portray Holiness? If not, change them to match the person God wants you to become; take care of your health by eating properly and exercising regularly. Have weight to gain or lose? Do it. Look inside, too: Can you see your goodness? Your integrity? Your trustworthiness? Your intelligence? If not, work on your inner qualities and reflect on what God wants you to become.

Scriptural Reading for the day:

Psalm 139:13-14 – "For You formed my inward parts; You wove me in my mother's womb. I will give thanks to You, for I am fearfully and wonderfully made; Wonderful are Your works, And my soul knows it very well."

DAY 17: THE ELECTRICITY OF TEAMWORK

Can two people walk together unless they agree? That is the word of God, and this principle works in our everyday lives. Our bodies run on electrical currents. God wants us to be in agreement before we can function together. Have you ever wondered why teams work so well together? That is because they agree and exchange currents: We receive charges into our systems from our teammates. Have you ever been hindered by a problem? And when you thought it through, it seems as if the solution to the problem is not forthcoming. And yet, when you voiced the problem to a friend who gave you his or her complete attention, the solution suddenly appears to you out of the blue, even without your friend having said a word? Well, that is the power of teamwork, because God allows them to agree with you. The energy from teamwork works together and thus creates an enabling environment for you to perform optimally.

Scriptural Reading for the day:

Leviticus 19:13,18: "Do not defraud your neighbor or rob him. [15] You shall do no injustice in judgment; you shall not be partial to the poor nor defer to the great, but you are to judge your neighbor fairly... [16]... and you are not to act against the life of your neighbor; I am the LORD. [18] You shall not take vengeance, nor bear any grudge against the sons of your people, but you shall love your neighbor as yourself; I am the LORD."

DAY 18: NETWORKING'S THE WAY TO GO

You've learned that God always provides someone for us to mentor us and that mentoring works. Also, you've learned that God's word says two people can only walk together unless they are in agreement, which forms the basis of teamwork. Now you come to find out that networking (meeting and working with people with like interests) works: Get involved in a community club, church group, political campaign, perhaps a sports group. Become a dues-paying member of a society whose focal point matches your career/life goals. Put your best foot forward and sincerely and honestly want to become an asset to the group(s). Networking is a form of how God wants us to spread our webs of connections with one another, and this can advance you to your goal while making you a better person.

Scriptural Reading for the day:

Psalm 133:1 – "How good and pleasant it is when God's people live together in unity!"

DAY 19: CREATE HARMONY — BANISH STRESS

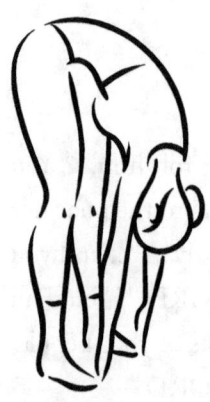

God's desire for our life is to be in harmony with all His creations. God personally created these natural gifts for our enjoyment and total wellbeing. Put yourself in touch with nature: Walk on the beach, in the park, down a country lane daily. Focus on the beauty around you, not in a passive way, but in a mindful way. Listen to a bird's song; notice the symmetry or asymmetry of a trees' silhouette, marvel at the majesty of an expanse of water, or a cloud filled sky. Total awareness of the beauty around you is a mini-vacation for your psyche and body: It takes you away from your immediate problems and provides a refreshing rest from the stress of your work-a-day world. It also makes you feel grateful for the gifts of nature. Pets have been known to bring harmony into people's lives too. Watching gold fish swim in their bowl or tank is a known stress reliever. Petting a cat asleep on your lap is one of the most soothing of pastimes. Being greeted exuberantly by your dog when you return home can only make you feel well loved and happy.

Scriptural Reading for the day:

Matthew 6:33 – "But seek first his kingdom and his righteousness, and all these things will be given to you as well. Therefore, do not worry about tomorrow, for tomorrow will worry about itself. Each day has enough trouble; of its own."

DAY 20: EXERCISE

Our total wellbeing is important for the services we render to God; because when we're fit and hearty we can serve Him better. The benefits of the exercise you do to become physically fit as part of this RHYTHM AND PATTERNS TO SUCCESS program will become self-evident as you incorporate them into your life along with a daily jog, walk or calisthenics. You will notice the sense of well-being that comes with getting your circulation going, becoming more flexible, toning up, and also the peace of mind that taking charge of your health and life brings. Choose a set of four to five calisthenics from this booklet, or maybe you have some exercises that you are more familiar with, if so, concentrate on making sure that you get a full-body work out each day don't compromise your health, (EXERCISE).

Scriptural Reading for the day:

Proverbs 17:22 – "A cheerful heart is a good medicine, but a crushed spirit dries up the bones."

I Corinthians 9:24 – "Do you not know that in a race all the runners run, but only one gets the prize? Run in such a way as to get the prize. Everyone who competes in the games goes into strict training. They do it to get a crown that will not last, but we do it to get a crown that will last forever."

DAY 21: MAKING OPPORTUNITIES OUT OF CRISIS

Life crisis are inevitable in this sinful world. Even Jesus experienced His while on earth, but in the end, he called on God for help. Ask yourself, what can you do to avoid life crisis without God? The answer to this would be absolutely nothing. So, if you can't avoid life crisis, don't allow yourself to regret the lost opportunity to make it right — but then go on to a positive outlook as you search for a solution to the crisis. One of the noble ways to handle this is to speak to your mentor or trusted friends for help. Sometimes, writing down the events that led up to the crisis will clarify at what point you could have changed the course of events. Remain hopeful; there is always a way. Every crisis provides us with the opportunity to come closer to God. This is life's way of helping us grow.

Scriptural Reading for the day:

Romans 8:28 – "And we know that in all things God works for the good of those who love him, who have been called according to his purpose."

DAY 22: GROW INTELLECTUALLY AND SPIRITUALLY

God wants us to grow spiritually and intellectually. He wants us to read and listen to the ways and forms He speaks to us. He'll open new doors for us if we can observe and learn. So, take new classes, learn new crafts, and broaden your interests: If you love listening to music, listen to soul edifying songs, and if you like urban songs, pay attention to music like jazz, rock, blues, and operas, too. If you love to read, consider faith-based books,

Activate God's Blessings

mysteries, romance novels, thrillers, read some Billy Grahm, Austin, Maugham, Maya Angelou, as well. Read about religions of the world and discuss them with your family or friends. Visit a different church or temple. Study a map of the world and memorize the new countries in Africa, the new names of major cities in China. Read poetry and summarize each poem in your own words. Note the poet's unique use  of words to convey meanings to you. Read scriptures daily before you go to sleep. Learn something new daily and commit it to memory. Be open to all things that are new to you.

Scriptural Reading for the day:

James 1:5 – "If any of you lacks wisdom, you should ask God, who gives generously to all without finding fault, and it will be given to you."

DAY 23: INCORPORATE CHARITY IN YOUR LIFE

 God loves a cheerful giver, and we must give with all sense of sincerity without expecting anything in return. So, when you give to others, you make a better world. Giving to national charities, — The Red Cross, Easter Seals, Salvation Army — helps those in times of crisis, ill health, natural disasters, and so much more. When we realize that we are our brother's keeper and act on that premise, then individuals, the community, and the church of God benefits. A suspension of judgment is often necessary to help the needy because God wants us to support each other. We do not always know what has brought down a brother or sister, but we do know that when a person is down, they must rise up, and frequently that is impossible

without our help. Charity, even in small acts like the godly act of the Shunammite women, adds to the world's goodness. Charity would never turn away from a person in dire need, and it would never be judgmental. Trying to emulate charity is a worthy goal and allows the soul to grow and become more.

Scriptural Reading for the day:

Proverbs 11:25 – "A generous person will prosper; whoever refreshes others will be refreshed."

DAY 24: YOU ARE A VALUED EMPLOYEE

Always look upon yourself as a value to the company that employs you. As a child of God, work to become the most outstanding in your department or area of expertise. Be attentive to what your boss or supervisor wants from your work. Be thorough, be neat, be helpful, and complete each project through to the end if that is what is expected of you, believing that God is taking notice of your hard-working attitude. He will promote you in due course. When you work hard, it not only gives you a sense of satisfaction and accomplishment, but your boss will know that he or she can rely on you for future assignments. Being reliable will give you a leg up on pending promotions. Be a pleasure to work with. Don't participate in idle gossip or chit-chat while at work. Speaking negatively of others is non-productive and mean spirited. If you want to rise in the company, ask your departmental head or human resources supervisor how to do so. Let it be known that you want to better yourself and grow with a company that you regard highly makes you promotional material. Think creatively. Believe in God, stand out as a team player, one who wants the company to succeed in its goals, and expect your promotion in due course.

Scriptural Reading for the day:

Colossians 3:23 – "Whatever you do, work at it with all your heart, as working for the Lord, not for men, since you know that you will receive an inheritance from the Lord as a reward. It is the Lord Christ you are serving."

Ephesians 4:28 – "…he must work, doing something useful with their own hands, that they may have something to share with those in need."

DAY 25: CREATE A STUDY HOUR

God doesn't want us to remain stagnant or complacent; He wants us to add value to our lives because that is when we can activate His blessings. So, create a study time in your creative environment space at home. Incorporate it into your daily routine. If you have a well-thought-out study plan, it will help you achieve goals. If you are taking a course at night school, a community college, a university, or a correspondence program, you will undoubtedly have a syllabus given to you by your teacher or professor. If you are pursuing a self-generated course of study, create your syllabus and tack it up on your study area bulletin board; include your booklist. Follow it. Be methodical. Goals are achieved by following a map that leads you to your destination. Your public library is one of the greatest resources and also online research.

Scriptural Reading for the day:

Proverbs 14:23 – "All hard work brings a profit, mere talk leads only to poverty."

DAY 26: PRACTICE AND REHEARSE

God wants us to exercise our faith and be practical in any situation. He wants us to see His likeness in us. So, when you take a look at yourself in the mirror, looking directly into your eyes and communicating your goals and plans out loud, God will help bring them to fruition. While you're there, be practical, and profess positive things to your life. Tell yourself that you are a good, kind, compassionate person with high ideals and that you love yourself. Tell yourself that you're on a journey that you anticipate will help you grow in the best ways possible. Make a list of your goals and practice stating them out loud and affirming that you will reach those goals. Tell yourself out loud that TO ACT THE MASTER IS TO BECOME THE MASTER. If you do this, you will give yourself permission and power to be the person God wants you to become. Permit others to become the person they want to become. Empowering yourself and validating others creates change for the better.

Scriptural Reading for the day:

2 Timothy 2:15 – "Do your best to present yourself to God as one approved, a worker who does not need to be ashamed and who correctly handles the word of truth."

DAY 27: CHOOSE YOUR WORDS WISELY

There is power in the words that come out of our mouth because, through word, God created the heavens and the earth, including all living creatures inhabiting it. One word spoken can affect a person for life in a good way or a bad way. Choose the good way. Words can create and shape the present and the future. The national bestseller, "The Power of Positive Thinking," incorporates positiveness into all phases of a person's life. Thinking positively allows a person to speak positively. Would you rather be around a nay-sayer or a person who radiates positiveness and hopefulness? We can choose to be negative or positive people. Have you noticed that the persons who at all times speak negatively have fewer friends and that they are avoided by others? Positive speaking and thinking do not mean you are being superficial. There is power in positive confession, and God is delighted with anyone that positively uses their tongue. When we see the good, we can see the way out of a difficult time in our lives. Always remember in any bad situation, there is a way out. Never give up. Keep in mind that things change. Polio was conquered. The Berlin Wall came down. Offer hope to others by your positive attitude.

Scriptural Reading for the day

Proverbs 7:1-3 – "My son, keep my words. And treasure my commandments within you. Keep my commandments and live, and my teaching as the apple of your eye. Bind them on your fingers; Write them on the tablet of your heart."

Psalms 35:28 – "My tongue will proclaim your righteousness, your praises all day long."

DAY 28: MAKE DECISIONS, TRUST INTUITION

A person that makes the right decision is a person that trusts God. As a rule of thumb: If you don't make decisions for yourself, someone else will make them for you. So, if you want to make the right decision, take it to God first and let Him direct your path. Seek godly counsel from your mentor, a trusted friend before making any decision. Keep in mind that a decision made is your responsibility: It is power in

action. Sometimes it helps to write down the pros and cons of going one way or another. Just seeing the advantages or disadvantages of a situation will sometimes clarify the problem in your mind: Instincts will show you which way to go. Often a decision has to be made quickly. Don't fear; trust God on your instincts — your intuition. Generally, intuitively, we know what the best course of action to take is. Just do it. No one has a perfect record. A decision made with God in control gives direction, stability, and the power to move ahead.

Scriptural Reading for the day

James 1:5 – " If any of you lacks wisdom, you should ask God, who gives generously to all without finding fault, and it will be given to you."

Proverbs 3:6 – "In all your ways submit to him, and he will make your paths straight."

DAY 29: FISCAL RESPONSIBILITY

One of the best ways to be financially disciplined is to seek godly counsel because God wants us to be responsible for everything, and not just in our finances. Know that God is the source of everything, and He is expecting you to be accountable to wherever your money goes. So, if you have to keep a daily diary, do so, at least for a while, until you can see a pattern of frugality or excesses. Create a budget and live within it. Try with all you might to put aside 5 or 10 percent of your monthly income until you have enough saved to tide you over for three to six months in case you should unexpectedly lose your job or are unable to work due to a health problem that might arise. Shop wisely; be a comparison shopper. Set goals for yourself: Make up your mind that when you have that three to six-month nest egg in place, you will begin a savings plan that will enable you to invest your money safely and wisely. Learn about interest-bearing savings accounts, annuities, CDs, stock portfolios and real estate. Never invest more than you can afford to lose. Diversify your investments. Be responsible. Going into debt unwisely or using credit cards, foolishly can bring sleepless nights. Loan money with the mental note that you may never get it back. It's better to give your friend money than to loan it. Stop using God's resources unwisely; He demands you to be financially accountable, so be accountable.

Scriptural Reading for the day

Philippians 4:19 – "And my God will meet all your needs according to the riches of his glory in Christ Jesus."

Deuteronomy 28:12 – "The LORD will open the heavens, the storehouse of his bounty, to send rain on your land in season and to bless all the work of your hands. You will lend to many nations but will borrow from none."

DAY 30: YOU ARE WHAT YOU THINK

Thinking is the beginning of all reality: Thoughts determine your words and actions. Let your imagination and thoughts be centered on the word of God — let it explore your options with an absolute fear of God — then refocus your vision while aiming for God's direction for your life. Feed your thought processes with positive thoughts and always take the high road with God accompanying you. Remember, you are what you think. And once more, so that it becomes a dominant power in your life: TO ACT THE MASTER IS TO BECOME THE MASTER.

Scriptural Reading for the day

Romans 8:15-17 – "For you have not received a spirit of slavery leading to fear again, but you have received a spirit of adoption as sons by which we cry out, "Abba! Father!" The Spirit Himself testifies with our spirit that we are children of God, and if children, heirs also, heirs of God and fellow heirs with Christ."

Setting Goals for Personal Development

The goal-setting form is a set of questions particularly tailored to meet your specific goal-setting needs. Your sincere answers to these questions will go a long way in actualizing your dreams, enhance your personal development, and ultimately activate God's blessings for your life. It will sharpen your skills as well as providing an enabling environment for your growth and development.

GOAL SETTING FORM

1. Give an overview of a set of goals you want to reach

   ....

2. What is the timeline for reaching these goals?

   ....

3. What will you do to make the environment ready for reaching your goals?

   ....

4. As you write down my plans, understand how important they are to your goals.

   ....

5. What are your best times for accomplishing these goals in your daily routine?

   ....

6. What will you do to keep a positive attitude as you work to achieve these goals?

   ....

7. What are some of the areas that you would like to build in your relationships?

   ....

8. What are some of the old habits that you would like to exchange for new ones?

   ....

9. What are some things that remind you of fear when you think about them?

   ....

10. God is the ultimate power in the universe that can help, how can you tap into his grace to activate his blessings in your life?

    ....

11. What can I do to build friendships and lasting relationships?

    ....

12. How can I build a better future by listening?

    ....

13. What relationship do I need to build, and how will I go about it?

   ....

14. Who will I get that is supportive of my dreams and visions?

   ....

15. Is there anyone that would work as a mentor who will be supportive of my plans?

   ....

16. What can I do to improve my personal being in grooming, weight and clothing?

   ....

17. Do I have members of a team or who I would choose to form a team?

   ....

18. What networks will I use, chamber of commerce groups, and or other community groups?

   ....

19. How will I use nature to lower stress?

   ....

20. What type of exercise program do I have to do to keep fit?

   ....

21. What are some of the things I will do to grow spiritually and intellectually?

   ....

22. Are there groups or individuals that I feel are drawn to help or support me?

   ....

23. If I work for a particular cooperation or I am self-employed, will I be fair either with an uncompromising commitment?

   ....

24. How much time will I give to education, and what GOAL do I have to reach it?

   ....

25. How will I project to myself and others that I can and will fulfill my desired outcome?

   ....

26. How will I use words to keep positive and plant verbal seeds to enhance my goals?

   ....

27. What can I do to be more in tune with everything around me, and how will I trust intuition?

   ....

28. What system will I use to manage my finances?

   ....

29. Whatever I want to accomplish, it can happen. How will I incorporate this into my plans?

   ....

Section Three

ACTIVATE GOD'S BLESSINGS THROUGH OUTREACH

We have all heard it said, "It is better to give than to receive," also, "God loves a cheerful giver." Scripture also says, "Give, and it shall be given, good measure and press down shall the Lord give to your bosom," these scriptures are absolutely right because giving is an act of sacrifice, and God values it. The ultimate gift that anyone can give or receive is his salvation, which is living for the Lord Jesus Christ. This section on outreach is filled with some great ideas on how to reach out to the needy, as well as helping others to find their purpose, while working on wining them to the Lord. It is no doubt that we all aspire to live a blessed life and also experience all God has promised us. I assure you that this is not done without developing oneself in Christ. We struggle to live a life without sickness, disappointment, intimidation, and financial imbalance. Still many Christians struggle to achieve all these, forgetting that in the Holy Book, God has handed us the key to unlocking His blessings; this is by taking delight in oneself with the Lord. Psalm 112:1 says, "Blessed are those who fear the LORD, who find great delight in his commands."

In other words, the bible has told you to build yourself by His will and be blessed. This book will teach you exactly how to achieve those blessings, in Psalm 133:3, we are told, "It is as if the dew of Hermon were falling on Mount Zion. For there, the LORD bestows His blessing, even life forevermore."

We are told that agreeing with the things of God makes us a candidate for His abundance. To "agree" means to "put to action," thus, blessing what the Lord wants to bless, causes immeasurable blessings. Looking at this carefully, we have heard of ordinary and extraordinary. The same way we incorporate statements like "the God of Abraham," "the God of Jacob, the God of David." Why is that? Because in our hearts we want the same experiences, and the same blessings granted to these men of God. The blessing I am sharing in this book is one that touches you and your generations, and this is the kind that Abraham and the others received.

We can also consider the transformation of Israel here, "The wilderness will rejoice and blossom. Like the crocus, it will burst into bloom," (Isaiah 35:1-2). We see that the nation was parched as no man's land; still, the Lord chose this nation and rebuilt it. In the old times, they prospered, and we see how today is no different. This proves to us that God can turn a desert into something great only if He is allowed in. It is simple, even if you feel that your situation seems unsolvable, I want you to know that God's specialty is turning rejected stones into head cornerstones. He is the only one who gives life to the dead and calls into being things that were not (Romans 4:17). In other words, he wants us to be more like Him. Our God is a King, and that makes us sons and daughters of a King. We being so, are given authority by using the word of God.

In the Old Testament, man was the first thing that God blessed. On the sixth day of creation, He proclaimed that man which He made in His image was very good, and He blessed the man and woman so that they may transfer this blessing. Look at this closely;

These are the instructions from God, and I will interpret this for us to understand God's initial plan for us.

- He said be Fruitful, meaning be productive.
- He said go and Multiply, meaning increase.
- He said Replenish, meaning use and restore also take and give.
- He said Subdue, meaning to rule, the ability for us to bind and loose.

God said this to Adam and Eve. He blessed them. God can bless you too, but we must first understand how to unlock these blessings, also how to preserve and keep them. Remember that as these blessings are given, they can also be taken. You may ask, how is this possible? I want us to look back at the time of creation. Satan, who came to visit Eve did not just come for the sole purpose of pushing them to disobey God. He came to steal their blessing, which was the power given to them by God, for them to rule the earth. If we also look at Esau and Jacob, though Jacob was a chosen generation by God, still, we saw that Esau felt robbed when the blessing was transferred to Jacob. What do I want us to learn from this? It is simple; as we go through the process of activating our blessings, we must also protect them, and must keep to the will of God.

I've had people tell me that this section of the book would be an excellent tool for pastors to have on their bookshelves; for some ideas about outreach. I feel like the Lord gave me this section of the book with all of its ideas as an inspiration to see the full body of Christ activated, going out and doing their part to win souls for the Lord. I remember meeting with one pastor showing him the ideas in the outreach section, and his reply to me was, "We are already doing a lot of these things."

I went through some of the areas of the book and asked, "If he had a team that went out and outreached all of them?" he said that he did from going to the hospital, visiting people at home, doing some of the variety of forms of outreach. My strong feeling is that this book will help to mobilize every single person in the church through prayers, motivating people to activate personal development while awaiting God's blessings for their lives. There's something for everyone to do as a part of reaching out, sharing the love of Jesus Christ with our peers, with our surroundings while influencing others on God's behalf.

Understanding The Concept Of Blessing

Blessing is the antonym of the word curse. Either a person is blessed or cursed. Not being blessed is also being cursed. Therefore either you are in the circle of life or the circle of death. Not choosing life (Jesus) is also the same as choosing death. The blessing I am teaching here is one that has been presented to us for a long time (since birth), it is ready-made and available to us, but we do not have its access. And not only can we not unlock these blessings, but we have not yet chosen to. A life outside blessing is one below God's original standard for us as true believers. The first step is to decide, and then, you activate. Thirdly, you maintain, and this automatically ends living below the standard of God's intentions.

We are aware that Jesus paid the price, meaning that it is our right as Christians and also a privilege that only the Heavenly Father can grant us. Like I said earlier, these blessings are already available because of the love He has for us. He never designed an oppressed life; this is the reason He gave His life so that we would have life abundantly. The idea was to set us free from sin and the captivity of Satan. In short, He has given us freedom and shown us the way to live, which is through Him, and through Him the blessing we desire can be activated.

Three ways to decipher God's blessing in relation to Him;

1. Acknowledge God As The Source Of All Blessings

Genesis 1:1 (The Hebrew translation) says, "In the beginning, THE BLESSED One created the heavens and the earth." Who is the blessed one? God is the blessed one, and this shows us that only the blessed can transfer blessings to others. A cursed person cannot bless another. A hungry person cannot feed another. God being Alpha and Omega (Revelation 1:8), means he is the source of everything in the world. He otherwise is the *'Blesser.'* He has promised, all that is left is to conceive His plan in our lives.

2. Seize the choice to be blessed.

See what God says, "This day I call the heavens and the earth as witnesses against you that I have set before you life and death, blessings and curses. Now choose life, so that you and your children may live." – Deuteronomy 30:19

Therefore whatever we choose, the repercussions will be counted to us. This means that partial Christians and unbelievers do not share this promise unless they return to Christ, because only through Christ can we seize the choice to be blessed. How do you choose life? You do this by honoring and obeying God, (Psalm 112:1.)

3. Following His Commandments Leads To Blessings

When I say commandments, I do not mean the tablets given to Moses by God – No, I mean every instruction the Lord laid for us in His Holy Book. We even see from the bible that, in the Old Testament, the children of God found it difficult to abide by the principles of God, which caused them to delay in reaching their blessings (40 years in the wilderness). All this was erased by the coming of Christ.

When Jesus came, He taught us another way to build a relationship with God. His teaching summed up the commandments of the Old Testament to one word – **LOVE** (Matthew 22:37-40). Jesus told us that the first commandment is to love the Lord our God with all of our heart, all of our soul, and all of our mind. Then He said the second is to "Love our neighbor as ourselves." If we say we love God, then we must love others because this is the commandment we were given by Jesus. To love, we must help one another and treat each other with care. Again to love, we must give.

How Giving Relates To God's Will

The act of giving is helping voluntarily without expectations, be it the future or after. It is governed by the thankfulness for the grace of God bestowed on the giver, which comes with greater blessings than the one initiated by the giver.

Giving eliminates greed. It is our nature to be frugal. We know that developing oneself in Christ is equivalent to self-abandonment. Giving incorporated into our daily lives can be used to break the chains of greed. How so? When we make this act regular, giving turns to pain in the flesh, this leads to the death of the flesh and a reborn in Christ. With the stake of greed broken, we are more Christ-like, and this is counted unto us as good work by God; thus, unleashing divine promises (2 Corinthians 9:9 & 1 Timothy 6:17-19)

Giving delights God. He is glorified by our act of giving and is pleased when praises and thanks are rendered to Him by the less privileged, especially when they have just received blessings from givers (2 Corinthians 9:11-12). If we become generous givers, we portray the character and nature of our Heavenly Father; this is the reason He says I love a cheerful giver (2 Corinthians 9:7). God has told us in Hebrews 13:16, "….do not forget to do good and to share with others, for with such sacrifices, God is pleased." This also proves that when we give, it delights God because we are providing to His creation and His work. Blessing mankind by solving problems like diseases, hunger, homelessness, nakedness, and poverty are all advances to the kingdom of God, so we ought to be a part of it.

Activate God's Blessings

Giving strengthens faith in God: Many people often say, "How can I give when I don't have enough?" Some fear running out of resources. But I want you to understand that true givers never lack because they have faith in God's divine provision. If we look at Luke 6:38 – "Give, and it shall be given to you." It shows that these true givers trust in the word of God; they do not worry about what they have left because they know it is the key. Faith is required for one to believe that a generous man will surely prosper just as those who scatter shall increase and be enriched. This principle is often perceived as a hoax to most people because they think the way to achieving blessings is to pile up all they have and hoard it. If at all we give, we do it only when a family member or friend is concerned. We must remember that everyone is God's people, no matter who they are. Giving requires faith, and when you give, your faith is strengthened, both are pleasing in the sight of God because He has told us in His book to give and also have faith in Him. (2 Corinthians 9:6-8, Hebrews 11:1, and Psalm 46:10).

Giving initiates God's intervention: The act of giving qualifies you for divine intervention. If we go back to the story of Dorcas – a giver without expectation, we are told she clothed the widows and then, one day, suddenly dies. We also see that these people whom she helped requested for the presence of Apostle Peter, who raises her from the dead. If Dorcas were a selfish woman, there would be no way for the intervention of God to be established in her life (Acts 9:36-43). We also see the blessings that followed the woman who gave her last oil to the prophet (1 Kings 17:12). Some times in life, we might demand something from God, but because we have not sown (giving) seeds into God's field, we cannot reap the blessing.

Years back, there was a wealthy man named John. D. Rockefeller. When he was around fifty-three years, he fell gravely ill. The illness was so terrible his doctors announced to him he had just a year to live. Upon hearing this, Mr. John Rockefeller changed his ways; he began to do good deeds, giving to the poor, churches, and schools. Surprisingly, he later died at the age of ninety-seven. This shows how God intervenes in the life of a giver. A giver who refreshes others will equally be refreshed. Christians who touch mankind also have touched heaven. I can confidently say, giving yields blessing (Proverbs 11:25) and covetousness and selfishness births curse (Proverbs 11:24b, 26).

To conclude, we must know that our Father does not judge what we give to the needy rather, His judgment is based on what we could have given (Genesis 4:2-8). I pray for everyone reading this book to receive the grace to be benevolent and the faith for God's provision in Jesus' Name, Amen.

There are so many simple things we can do that we do not even think as a form of outreach, using our telephones to call as an outreach, joining a service club, or even targeting someone at the bank that you can go to regularly. Deliberately becoming a little league coach or a member of a service club organization within your community will go a long way in lifting people out of a hopeless situation. Using the church to put on a business meeting as a tool for looking at reaching out to one's community is another form of outreach that we can use to help those in a dire situation.

There are so many different ways that we can utilize outreach and be valid for the kingdom of God. My sincere desire is as we seek God in prayer, giving our praises to God, and building ourselves up with our personal development guide, we'll be inspired to reach out to others and be of service to God. Through outreach, we'll see the great move of God among our communities, our friends, our state, nation, and the world

Helping With The Newborn As An Outreach

God Almighty is the great giver of life, and we shouldn't forget that. Helping families with newborns is a great way to share the gospel because they are thinking about the health and welfare of their child. While the heart is open, give them gifts, but don't forget the greatest gift of all: Jesus Christ, our Savior.

What can you do to further the course?

- You can take flowers to the mother and her baby: Blessing people with flowers is one of the most beautiful gifts you can gift someone. Their roles in our lives transcend human comprehension. When you give a new mom flowers, their mood becomes heightened, and sometimes things become appealing to them. If you want to convey your deepest emotion of love to new moms, consider giving them beautiful flowers.
- Make a meal for the new mom and her family: Making a meal for new moms doesn't mean they are hungry or depending on you for food. It simply indicates the depth of your love and compassion for them. This is what God commanded us to do, that we should love without condition. A good meal or hot soup will go a long way in soothing their taste buds and relieving them from birth-related stress.
- Take a gift of diapers, baby wipes, shampoo, and baby oil: When you give newborn babies gifts, you are practically helping the family to offset some financial burdens. Thus, they can save more for the baby's future needs, and in turn, you are practically invoking God's blessing upon yourself because they are God's heritage.
- Give greeting cards or books about new babies: Greeting cards and books that talk about babies will go a long way in helping new moms in many special ways; greeting cards depict your essence of love and sense of belonging. When you give them books that talk about newborns, you are practically contributing to the growth and development of the newborn child.

Share Compassion Within the Framework of These Ideas

- Offer to help the mom. Talk about the health and the future success of the child. Encourage them to consider raising their child in the Lord's way.
- Give a baby book from a Christian author. Write a note in your card of how God's blessing has come to them. Invite them to a baby dedication.

Scriptures that Speak for Newborn

Psalm 127:3 – "Children are a heritage from the LORD, offspring a reward from him. Like arrows in the hands of a warrior are children born in one's youth. Blessed is the man whose quiver is full of them. They will not be put to shame when they contend with their opponents in court."

Psalm 139:13-16 – "For you created my inmost being; you knit me together in my mother's womb. I praise you because I am fearfully and wonderfully made; your works are wonderful, I know that full well. My frame was not hidden from you when I was made in the secret place. When I was woven together in the depths of the earth, your eyes saw my unformed body. All the days ordained for me were written in your book before one of them came to be.

Helping The Homeless As An Outreach

Jesus had no place on earth that he could call home; in fact, he didn't even want it to be his home. The apostle Paul often talked about leaving "this place" to be in his home, a place considered to be a better place than his earthly abode. Many homeless people do not have this hope and are in despair. God's heart aches for these people. Here are some ways that we can reach out in the grace of the Lord to the homeless:

- If a brother or sister in the Lord is homeless, you can give them a place to stay, whether it is a hotel room or staying with you. If single, the same gender should stay together.
- Help a poor, wandering stranger find a place to stay. Pray about it to see if it should be with you, in a hotel, or a shelter. When you take helpless and hopeless people off the street, you have practically reduced their chances of exposure to social vices.
- Volunteer to work at a shelter: It doesn't necessarily have to be money all the time. The Lord has equipped you with some skills that can be useful for His kingdom; so, utilize your skills and don't hide them. This way, people tend to believe you value them and that you place premium attention to their total well-being.
- a homeless person out to eat: When you take a homeless person to eat with you, then you have given them the hope to live for another day, and it means you have fulfilled what the Lord said in the book of Matthew 25:35. Find a nice restaurant and let your company eat his/her favorite menu without restriction. Make him/her feel comfortable!

Share Compassion Within the Framework of These Ideas

- Help create a plan to bring a homeless person to sustainable living conditions, using biblical principles. Ask questions to show your concern about how they ended up on the streets, and share with them the better home prepared for us in heaven through Christ.
- Take a homeless person out to eat and talk about a plan for life restoration and salvation.
- Ask that person the one thing he or she would want if he or she could have it, and show them how Christ wants to help them activate His blessings for their lives.

The scripture that Speaks for the Homeless

Matthew 25:35-40 – "⁵ For I was hungry and you gave me something to eat, I was thirsty and you gave me something to drink, I was a stranger and you invited me in, I needed clothes and you clothed me, I was sick and you looked after me, I was in prison and you came to visit me.' "Then the righteous will answer him, 'Lord, when did we see you hungry and feed you, or thirsty and give you something to drink? When did we see you a stranger and invite you in, or needing clothes and clothe you? When did we see you sick or in prison and go to visit you?' "The King will reply, 'Truly I tell you, whatever you did for one of the least of these brothers and sisters of mine, you did for me."

Helping The Widows As An Outreach

In James 1:27, God tells us to consider the widows and care for them. When we are doing our part in this regard, we are helping God fulfill His desire for these hurting people. Allow the Lord to activate His blessings in your life by partaking in this form of outreach, and you will be blessed in return. Here are some suggestions for the widow outreach:

- Take them a bag of food or a gift certificate: Food is essential for our survival, and it is one of the basic commodities of life. No matter how small it is, a hungry person will always appreciate your act of love when you provide them food whenever he/she is hungry.
- Give a gift of clothing for a child: To lose someone you love passionately could be dehumanizing, and that's why as Christians, we have to take every necessary step in grieving with the widows and cater to the child/children of the deceased. You can do this by visiting stores and get some nice clothes for them. It doesn't have to be expensive, just make sure they are neat, appealing to the eyes, and wearable.

- Talk to widows about their interests; help them investigate things to do, such as taking a class at a junior college. Listen when they share memories of their spouse, and help them journey through their process of recovery.

Share Compassion Within the Framework of These Ideas

- Take her/him (widow) to an event he/she is interested in. Whenever appropriate, use examples from the scripture about that situation.
- Buy her/him a good cookbook, health book, or other subjects written by Christians that can help them in coping with stress and grief.

Scriptures that Speak for the widows

James 1:27 – "Religion that God our Father accepts as pure and faultless is this: to look after orphans and widows in their distress and to keep oneself from being polluted by the world."

Proverbs 15:25 – "The LORD tears down the house of the proud but he sets the widow's boundary stones in place."

Helping With Food As An Outreach

While the Holy Spirit feeds and strengthens our hungry souls, one of the necessities of life is that we also feed our bodies with nourishing foods. Jesus fed people as he ministered to them; some even followed Him just because of the food. Think about the number of people who must have accepted Him as their personal savior because they heard him speak while He was performing His own Food Outreach for the multitudes. People often share their food when they grow a garden, raise animals, or otherwise have a plentiful amount to share, although food can be shared at any time in the form of a gift certificate, a bag of groceries, or in many other ways.

You may know of a family or person who really needs food, and whatever you do, ensure no family or anybody goes hungry around you.

You want to assist those in hunger and thirst, here are some suggestions on how you can minister to the needy through food outreach:

- Start a food drive at your work, your church, or in your neighborhood: A great way to do this is to look for people of like-minds that share your vision and passion of feeding those in need of food. There is a saying that goes, "There is strength in numbers." By doing this, you can reach a wide range of targeted needy within a short time.
- Take food to the local shelter and set aside a day to research those around you who may have a need. Do this by developing a group of people that you can help, whether friends, relatives, or others who may be in need. Your little act of love counts! Make it count.
- Take a day once a week or once a month and invite someone over for a meal that you think might need food. There is this sense of satisfaction that comes along with sharing meals with someone, and this sometimes creates an avenue for over-the-meal discussion. Who knows, it might be an avenue to talk about faith-related perspectives.

Share Compassion Within the Framework of These Ideas

- Set some time aside for taking someone out to lunch; share the gospel. As you share, do this not for yourself but for Christ. also, help them to develop a biblical plan of sustainability while moving toward self sufficiency.
- Don't give up on them if it takes longer than you anticipated. This can be a great time for ministry. Talk about any experiences you've had with hunger. Talk about how Jesus fed the people and had compassion on them.

The scripture that Speaks for those in need of Food

James 2:15-17 – "Suppose a brother or a sister is without clothes and daily food. If one of you says to them, 'Go in peace; keep warm and well fed,' but does nothing about their physical needs, what good is it? In the same way, faith by itself, if it is not accompanied by action, is dead."

Psalm 136:25 – "He gives food to every creature. His love endures forever."

Helping With Tutoring and Developing Personal Skills As An Outreach

Many people don't have the skills needed to succeed in today's complex and changing world. Tutoring is a great way to help. We can offer our skills in teaching math, computers, personal developmental skills, or even teach how to read the word of God; the list is long. The Bible tells us to let everything we do, be unto the glory of God. Helping one person to learn how to read will also encourage another person with the potential to read the word of God.

The Lord will reward you both for carrying out His mandate for activating the blessings meant for us as a child of God. How can you help in this ministry?

- Set up a tutoring program in your church for kids. One of the best ways to help is to equip kids with the skills needed to enhance their productivity. Take opinion samples of where their interests lie and come up with tutoring plans that will make them better for society and ultimately God.
- Set up an ESL program for non-English speaking people: English Language is often a barrier to non-speaking English people, and this is a great avenue to come with a message of hope. Try to set

up a literacy program for adults with other volunteers that share your vision and passion. Another way is to volunteer as a music tutor for adults and children.

- Teach a cooking class: Food is life, and life is food! A cooking class is a great way to share experience and impart skills, and the beauty of it is that it doesn't require too much money to set up. You can make it a weekend class where people will be opportune to learn different methods of cooking.

Share Compassion Within the Framework of These Ideas

- Give a class on foods from scriptures and have an international food tasting party at your home or church and invite people to the party who are comfortable with sharing the gospel of Christ.

Scriptures that Speak for Tutoring

1 Corinthians 4:17 – "For this reason I have sent to you Timothy, my son whom I love, who is faithful in the Lord. He will remind you of my way of life in Christ Jesus, which agrees with what I teach everywhere in every church."

Psalm 32:8 – "I will instruct you and teach you in the way you should go; I will counsel you with my loving eye on you."

Helping Public Schools & College As An Outreach

There are many issues that students have to deal with on a daily basis, and one of this is peer pressure. It is a powerful agent that can lead us all into destructive behavior if not effectively managed – school and college-age people are particularly susceptible to this vice. However, if we plant the seeds of encouragement and embrace Christ's love in it, this can be an area where we can harvest many souls for God's kingdom. Young people are always proactive and creative if they are equipped with the necessary skills. When the word of God penetrates your heart and in turn, touches their hearts at school or on the college campus, they will manifest their true potential. Here are some ways to start planting those seeds:

- Invite a friend to your youth group or youth outing, such as a ski trip, bowling, skating, etc. Get them together to study a specific subject. Take a class together, such as exercise, music, or join the same club that is combined with the responsibilities of sharing the good news of Christ, or that is mainly Christian based.
- Start a campus club; this could be for homework, games, or just a friend's club, and don't forget to give them a friendship gift.

Share Compassion Within the Framework of These Ideas

- Find the time when you can talk about what you both believe in, then you can share your belief in Christ. Invite your friend to youth night at your church. Recommend a Christian playlist to listen to in the genre of music that they would like.
- Start a conversation about your friend's future, and ask questions such as, "Where do you hope to be when you get out of school?" Let the conversation be centered on ways they can activate their God-given potential; and ultimately how it can lead them to eternal life in Christ.

Scriptures that Speak for Public School

2 Timothy 2:22 – "Flee the evil desires of youth, and pursue righteousness, faith, love, and peace, along with those who call on the Lord out of a pure heart."

Titus 2:6-7 – "Likewise urge the young men to be sensible; in all things show yourself to be an example of good deeds, *with* purity in doctrine..."

Helping The Elderly As An Outreach

Ministering to the elderly is a very special and rewarding area of outreach. The elderly in our society often have special needs and require tender love and care. In performing your elderly outreach, pray for the leading of the Holy Spirit to see what focus the Lord would lead you to. Pray that God would show you when and how the gospel should be shared. As you prayerfully minister and give yourself to this outreach, God will bless you and give to them the most important thing: salvation.

Having a passion for the care of older people around you, here are some suggestions on how you can help:

- Elderly people are sometimes fragile people that need assistance. A great way to assist them is to offer to mow the lawn for them, do handy work around the house for them, and ask if you can pray with them to strengthen their faith.
- Also, you can assist by reading their mail to them and offer to help them write letters if they ever need help in such regards.
- Take a cooked meal, give them flowers, and sometimes, just a simple visit can be very special in their lives. You can also volunteer to give them a ride to the store to shop, when they have medical appointments, or here's a thought: Take them to church!

Share Compassion Within the Framework of These Ideas

- Get to know them on a personal level. Then you can share the gospel more confidently. This will show that you care. Use your special holidays to give them gifts that focus on Christ.

- Consider the time that this person may have before they go to be with their maker. Discuss their beliefs in Christ, show them the way to holiness, and give them your spiritual understanding of Christ's love.

Scriptures that Speak for Elderly

1 Timothy 5:1-2 – "Do not sharply rebuke an older man, but *rather* appeal to *him* as a father, *to* the younger men as brothers, the older women as mothers, *and* the younger women as sisters, in all purity."

Leviticus 19:32 – "Stand up in the presence of the aged, show respect for the elderly and revere your God. I am the LORD."

Helping On The Telephone As An Outreach

Everything can be used for the glory of God, even the telephone. Use it skillfully and effectively, and God will use you to bring peace, joy, and healing to a lost or hurting soul.

Here are a few suggestions for starting a telephone outreach:

- Our telephone is one of the great tools we can use for winning souls for Christ. You can start by making a list of people to call once per week. Discuss anything you like. The objective is to create a connection with someone who may need encouragement or to talk to a friend.
- Call a senior once a week to encourage them and offer companionship, and do not exclude your family members or friends. Check on their well-being, and don't forget to pray with them on the phone.

Share Compassion Within the Framework of These Ideas

- The key to sharing the gospel on the phone is being sensitive, knowing when to share, and, just as importantly, how long to share. The goal is to move them along with the gospel when you can do so. You can end your conversation with, "God bless you."
- Read scripture over the phone to friends, the sick, elderly, and to people whom the Holy Spirit leads you to share this with. Quote a scripture or a word of wisdom on your voice mail.

Scriptures that Speak for Telephone

1 Peter 4:11 – "If anyone speaks, they should do so as one who speaks the very words of God. If anyone serves, they should do so with the strength God provides, so that in all things God may be praised through Jesus Christ. To him be the glory and the power for ever and ever, Amen."

Col 4:6 – "Let your conversation be always full of grace, seasoned with salt, so that you may know how to answer everyone."

Helping Those In Grief As An Outreach

Sometimes one of the best ways to reach others is to offer comfort and compassion to those who are going through a tough time. Loss of a loved one is one of the most difficult situations in life, and one thing to keep in mind is that God wants to take care of those who are left behind. Handle them as God would and look for ways to share the faith of the gospel with them. How can you further the course?

- Find people through the newspapers who have lost a loved one and send a card with an encouraging note. Reach out to those with terminal illnesses, and comfort people you know who have lost a loved one.

- Pain is sometimes difficult to deal with; it weakens one's spirit and causes instability of one's faith in Christ. A woman that just suffered a miscarriage needs to be supported, and she needs comfort to get through her grief. Be there for her because your words of encouragement will go a long way in comforting her.
- Reach out to those stricken with misfortune or hardship: A little act of kindness is all that you need to extend God's love. Pray with them with scriptural backings and assure them of new hope in Christ Jesus.

Share Compassion Within the Framework of These Ideas

- Take food to the family. Keep in touch with them: Minister to their needs using the scriptures. Pray for the grieving person or family, and offer to be there for them as a support.

Scriptures that Speak for Those in Grief

Lamentations 3:32 – "Though he brings grief, he will show compassion, so great is his unfailing love."

Isaiah 60:20 – "Your sun will never set again, and your moon will wane no more; the LORD will be your everlasting light, and your days of sorrow will end."

Helping With Job/Employee As An Outreach

The workplace often presents a great opportunity for outreach. It is one of the places where we readily make new friends, even build close relationships. Our co-workers are around us for up to eight hours each day, which offers us plenty of time to know them, to discuss many different things, and how to be a living example of a Christ filled life that can activate God's blessings for their lives. There are many outreach and fellowship opportunities while on the job. Here are just a few examples of how you can key into the ministry:

- Find people with interests similar to yours and then develop a cordial friendship with them. Keep a lookout for job openings and encourage them to learn vocational skills while awaiting God's provision for jobs.
- A great place of initiating a godly association is to start a club: golf, bowling, basketball, investment, writing, with a friend or persons of like-minded perspectives. Ensure that the objectives and mission statement behind this idea is Christ-aligned.
- Take a person to lunch each week and invite them to a Christian function related to something of their interest.

Share Compassion Within the framework of These Ideas

- Be there when a co-worker is in crisis and ensure you give them Jesus' perspective on the issue they are currently facing.
- Get together with another Christian for a session, game, or event related to a subject that would interest all parties, and use it as a chance to share the gospel.

Scriptures that Speak for Job/Employee

Ephesians 4:28 – "…he must work, doing something useful with their own hands, that they may have something to share with those in need."

Colossians 3:23 – "Whatever you do, work at it with all your heart, as working for the Lord, not for men, since you know that you will receive an inheritance from the Lord as a reward. It is the Lord Christ you are serving."

Helping With Those in Businesses As An Outreach

Sometimes it is hard to think of how you can share your faith in Jesus with your peers or fellow business acquaintances. But whatever we do, let us do it unto the glory of God, and that includes our business endeavors. It is He who has given us our business, and it is He who will prosper and sustain it. Our ethics and ways of doing business will speak loud for themselves. We must cultivate the habit of exhibiting constant prayer life and be creative in whatever we do. Let the Lord lead you with your business outreach. Here's how you can help:

- If you are an expert in a business that your friends or neighbors are currently undertaking, then it is an avenue to build a relationship with them. Offer assistance in forms of advice, take them to lunch or breakfast once a week, and if it becomes a conducive avenue for initiating faith talks, please do not allow the opportunity to slide.
- Always look for tips on how to improve their business; discuss investments, future growth, or marketing strategies; also, join the Chamber of Commerce and other service clubs where your voice in the business community can be heard.
- Becoming an expert in your field will also gain their trust. Invest in your personal growth and development.

Share Compassion Within the Framework of These Ideas

- Talk about Biblical principles on business to show that God is concerned about our businesses succeeding. Invite your coworkers to meet other Christian business people excelling in their niche.
- Put on a workshop with your church that can benefit businesses such as marketing, web design, investment, or others, and have a successful Christian business person talk about his or her relationship with the Lord.

Scriptures that Speak for Business

Psalm 128:1-2 – "How blessed is everyone who fears the LORD, Who walks in His ways. When you shall eat of the fruit of your hands, You will be happy and it will be well with you."

Deuteronomy 28:12-13 – "The LORD will open for you His good storehouse, the heavens, to give rain to your land in its season and to bless all the work of your hand; and you shall lend to many nations, but you shall not borrow. The LORD will make you the head and not the tail, and you only will be above, and you will not be underneath, if you listen to the commandments of the LORD your God, which I charge you today, to observe *them* carefully."

Helping With Those in Prison/ Jail As An Outreach

Prison outreach can be an effective way to minister and spread the gospel to those who are often turned away by society. However, God loves both the innocent and the guilty alike and wants us to share the gospel with everyone, regardless of their disposition. Apostle Paul, along with many of Jesus' disciples, had a very dynamic and effective ministry from within jails and won many souls to Christ. When we minister to people in prison, let us do so through the love of Jesus Christ that has the power to save and heal. Ensure you pray for the prisoner's children and their spouse. Having an urge to minister to those in prison or jail, here is how you can help:

- Sometimes, we may have the call to go to prisons or jails to help people or to minister to a person but, if we minister to their families, we are helping them.
- Give a bag of food, clothing for the children, or paying a bill that can help them in this time of need, both spiritually and financially.

- Send letters of hope to prisoners, (men to men, and women to women), and send a letter or card to their loved ones. You can volunteer to go into the jail to teach a class, play music, or use other skills you may have that may be of service.

Share Compassion Within the Framework of These Ideas

- Start a jail outreach or join one through your church or a Christian group within your community. Help with study materials from the scriptures that can hasten their personal development.
- Become a mentor for a child whose parent is in jail and invite them to church with you: When you mentor a child, such a child is capable of developing more self-confidence, high self-esteem, and can create and achieve bigger goals.

Scriptures that Speak for those in Prison/Jail

Matthew 25:35 – "For I was hungry, and you gave me food, I was thirsty, and you gave me something to drink, I was a stranger, and you invited me in, I was naked, and you gave me clothing, I was sick, and you took care of me, I was in prison, and you visited me."

Psalms 68:5 – "A father to the fatherless, a defender of widows, is God in his holy dwelling. God sets the lonely in families; he leads forth the prisoners with singing: but the rebellious live in a sun-scorched land."

Helping With People Living on the Street As An Outreach

When we are conducting our personal outreach ministry, we need to remember to "Go into the highways and byways to spread the gospel," (Luke 14:23). This scripture refers to the fact that everyone needs God's love and a personal relationship with Christ. While it is good to have special needs groups as part of our outreach plan, the homeless, elderly, pregnant teens, we can't forget to minister to the rest of the world. When you look at the people on the "highways and byways," remember to be the salt of the earth that the Lord would have you be. Here is what you can do to help:

- People living on the street are vulnerable to all form of social vices, and as a way of outreach, you can help them find a place you feel comfortable with, a coffee shop, restaurant, or bakery, for example, and get to know some of the people that hang out there.
- You can also create a routine plan on how to know some of the street people around you, and talk one-on-one with them. Buy them a cup of coffee.
- Offer to create a plan to help them get off the street, and ride in public transit with them while engaging them in a constructive discussion. Do not forget to help them with what they can participate in, this can either be a vocational skill or even passive income ideas.

Share Compassion Within the Framework of These Ideas

- Create a plan that includes God's desire to bring them to a life of hope and restoration: This is particularly important because the sole aim of engaging in outreach is to draw the hopeless and even the hopeful to Christ.
- Ride public transit to meet people and talk to them about their experience. Talk about your spiritual life in Christ, and invite them to participate in community support groups.

Scriptures that Speak for Street People

Matthew 22:9-10 – "Go therefore to the main highways, and as many as you find *there,* invite to the wedding feast. Those slaves went out into the streets and gathered together all they found, both evil and good; and the wedding hall was filled with dinner guests."

Mark 16:15 – "He said to them, "Go into all the world and preach the good news to all creation."

Helping With Those in Your Neighborhood As An Outreach

Allow the Lord to lead you in outreach to a neighbor. This can sometimes be difficult, but if done tactfully, it can be a very successful and rewarding opportunity. Being prayerful is number one. Make it your goal to see the whole neighborhood saved for the sake of Christ. You can draw from many areas of the outreach sections using different concepts of outreach for children, elderly, sports, and more. Just ask God to lead you, and He will. Here is how you can start:

- Invite a neighbor over for dinner and discuss the possibility of setting up a neighborhood watch or other programs that may be needed in your area. This forms a basis of mutual relationships and encourages community participation.
- Organize a block party and create a neighborhood club or a neighborhood association that will focus on areas such as beautifying, legal matters, restoration, or anything else you may come up with.

Share Compassion Within the Framework of These Ideas

- When you get to know your neighbors' hobbies, you're developing a platform for sharing your faith in Christ while ensuring their growth and development. Have a block party and invite some of your Christian friends as guests.

- Discuss ways to succeed in family life, with children, or in marriage, and give them scriptures that'll build their foundation while at the same time showing them the process to success.

Scriptures that Speak for Neighborhood

Leviticus 19:18 – "You shall not hate your fellow countryman in your heart; you may surely reprove your neighbor, but shall not incur sin because of him. 'You shall not take vengeance, nor bear any grudge against the sons of your people, but you shall love your neighbor as yourself; I am the LORD."

Helping With The Ministry Of Writing As An Outreach

If you like to write, then you may want to count yourself as a scribe, called to good works in Christ Jesus, to inspire, encourage, aid, and serve the Lord through letter writing. Biblical scribes helped some of the apostles write the scriptures; their talents were used for God, and yours can be, too. Rejoice in the Lord for the ability to write. Let your voice be heard through this ministry! Your pen might be the voice that will set those in bondage free. Here are ways you can minister:

- you are a wordsmith, this is an opportunity to evangelism, and you can start by writing faith-related articles, journals, letters, emails, to your newspapers or blogs; you can even send in letters or emails to the editors and even publishers.
- Another way to evangelize the good news of Christ is to start writing letters to people in the hospital, prison, jail, and convalescent homes. You can extend this act of outreach to seniors who can no longer write by writing their letters for them.

Share Compassion Within the Framework of These Ideas

- Go to a poetry reading with a friend with the purpose of sharing the gospel, an example of a place to go is where others are sharing their written work.
- Put on an event at your church or in a community hall. Invite your friends, those that enjoy writing, and if possible, have a professional author speak.

Scriptures that Speak for Letter Writing

Proverbs 7:1-3 – "My son, keep my words and treasure my commandments within you. Keep my commandments and live, And my teaching as the apple of your eye. Bind them on your fingers; Write them on the tablet of your heart."

Psalms 45:1 – "My heart is stirred by a noble theme as I recite my verses for the king: my tongue is the pen of a skillful writer."

Helping Through Sports As An Outreach

1 Corinthians 9:24 says, "Run in such a way as to get the prize." Sports outreach can be challenging but can also be very rewarding. Not only will sports activities help us to remain healthy, but participation in sports allows us to meet new people and create new friendships, which gives us a new opportunity for outreach in the community. Listed below are some sports outreach activities. With God, "All things are possible to them that believe," let the Lord direct you, and be of good courage. Having an urge of the Spirit of God to minister to people through sports? Here is what you can do:

- Sports are a great way to initiate a mutual relationship and even enforce community participation in things that matter. You can

use this avenue to start winning souls for Christ by either starting a neighborhood league team and join a community team; by doing this, you can start giving out faith-related tracts after games.
- Create a team with any sports and mix the team with community people and people that are believers of Christ. In this case, grab any opportunity that presents itself and win souls for Christ.

Share Compassion Within the Framework of These Ideas

- Go to ball games with a friend with the purpose of sharing the gospel, an example of a place to begin is where Monday Night Football is playing.
- Put on an event at your church or in a community hall. Invite your sports friends, and If possible, have a pro sports figure speak.

Scriptures that Speak for Sports

Hebrews 12:1-2 – "Therefore, since we have so great a cloud of witnesses surrounding us, let us also lay aside every encumbrance and the sin which so easily entangles us, and let us run with endurance the race that is set before us, [2] fixing our eyes on Jesus, the author and perfecter of faith, who for the joy set before Him endured the cross, despising the shame, and has sat down at the right hand of the throne of God."

I Corinthians 9:24 – "Do you not know that in a race all the runners run, but only one gets the prize? Run in such a way as to get the prize. Everyone who competes in the games goes into strict training. They do it to get a crown that will not last, but we do it to get crowns that will last forever."

Helping Through Music As An Outreach

It has been said that music is like medicine. However, music also has the power to break down the barriers that may stand in the way of sharing

God's word. Throughout the ages, music has been used virtually in every culture, and it can be a very powerful tool for spreading the gospel, tutoring, giving lessons, or singing at a hospital or home. Let the Lord lead you in this outreach, and be blessed while you bless others. Here is how you can help:

- Play music at a convalescent or retirement home: Music is an excellent way of uplifting one's soul in times of loneliness and depression. You can start by writing Christian songs with powerful lyrics of hope in Christ, play it for people in the convalescent or retirement home.
- Play music to those on the street and those in jail; these people are no exception to the message of hope in Christ. Sometimes you can do this with people that share your vision and passion; there is strength in numbers, so make use of it. Rehearse together and pray together for the Holy Spirit to guide and rest on you.

Share Compassion Within the Framework of These Ideas

- Write songs that convey Christ's messages of hope, sing them at events, and to those who are hospitalized.
- Play in a group that won't compromise your faith, and use it as a way to share the gospel of Christ.

Scriptures that Speak for those in Music outreach

Psalm 32:7 – "You are my hiding place; you will protect me from trouble and surround me with songs of deliverance."

Psalm 33:1-3 – "Sing for joy in the LORD, O you righteous ones; praise is becoming to the upright. Give thanks to the LORD with the lyre; sing praises to Him with a harp of ten strings. Sing to Him a new song; play skillfully with a shout of joy."

Helping Through the Media As An Outreach

These are just some basic ways of getting the word out about the name of Jesus. It is said that the name of Jesus has the power to heal, to save, and to keep us in a sound mind. Use the name whenever possible, and let the name work for itself. How can you function in this ministry?

- Write letters to the editor. Call in on talk shows that interest you, and create a press conference about outstanding people, good deeds, a grandparent's 100th birthday, or a special holiday.
- Put flyers out in various places with positive messages on them and have business cards printed with your message of hope about Christ on them.

Share Compassion Within the Framework of These Ideas

- Put on some Jesus Loves You events; they don't have to be huge events, your sole objective is that you are getting the name out there, and you are spreading the gospel. Make the message of invitation on your card to share in the love of Christ.
- Flyers can be very powerful in explaining the love of Christ and offer help. Be sure to put your email address on the flyer. Pray for an editor or a particular broadcast celebrity, and let them know you are doing so.

Scriptures that Speak for Media

Luke 10:1&17 – "After these things, the Lord appointed seventy-two others and sent them two by two ahead of him to every town and place where he was about to go. The seventy-two returned with joy and said, Lord, even the demons submit to us in your name."

Matthew 9:35-38 – 'Jesus was going through all the cities and villages, teaching in their synagogues and proclaiming the gospel of the kingdom, and healing every kind of disease and every kind of sickness. [36.] Seeing the people, He felt compassion for them, because they were distressed and dispirited like sheep without a shepherd. [37.] Then He said to His disciples, "The harvest is plentiful, but the workers are few. [38.] "Therefore beseech the Lord of the harvest to send out workers into His harvest."

Helping Through The Internet As An Outreach

Jesus said that we would do greater things than He did. This is hard to imagine; however, we have so many different ways of sharing the good news today than we've ever had before, and surely there will be many more to come. The Internet is one tool that we should use as much as possible, such as in sharing links, sending greetings, writing notes of encouragement to others – the possibilities are endless! But most of all, let it be a tool for spreading the word of God. If you're not the talking type, this medium is a great way to spread the gospel of hope to the people around you. Here's how you can reach out:

- The internet has become one of the greatest miracles of the last two decades, and it has become a useful tool that can be used to reach many people around the world. To start with, you can join a special-interest newsgroup, a YouTube channel, social media, or create an online newsletter for your friends or family. You can even start a newsgroup by doing an internet search on how to start one.
- You can develop an extensive address book and create special groupings to be able to send links and special messages and cards to them. To reach a broader audience, you can create a great web site that you can advertise and link traffic to.

Share Compassion Within the Framework of These Ideas

- When you send an email, add a Christian link to your page to plant a seed within this person. Create a web site that would also be interesting to non-Christians; include links or Christian banners that share the gospel.
- If you start a newsgroup, make it known that you are a Christian, even though it may be subject to a professional topic in your trade. This is a great way to spread the name of Jesus.

Scriptures that Speak for Internet

Matthew 4:19 – "Come, follow me," Jesus said, "and I will send you out to fish for people."

Helping Those With Health Issues As An Outreach

The Lord wants every one of us to prosper through good health. Helping someone with health issues for the sake of the gospel is a noble cause. If you are in good health and live a healthy lifestyle, you can share your knowledge and set an example for those around you so that others may also enjoy the healthy life that God desires for us. Here are some suggestions on how you can be of help:

- God has placed you in good health because He wants you to assist others, He wants to activate His blessings of others through you, and He wants others to enjoy His benefits of divine health. As a way to start, you can invite a friend to do a workout with you, create a health support group, and invite professionals to educate people on how to live a healthy life.

- Do a study about a health topic with a friend, join an offline or online group together or another no-cost activity, and share scriptures that refer to topics on health.

Share Compassion Within the Framework of These Ideas

- Create a survey of what this person wants from life, and wherever you see an opening for the gospel, plant the seed without hesitation.
- Once you have gotten to know this person, invite them to a Christian function they may have an interest in. Fast together for cleansing, discuss Bible context on fasting, and the benefits and promises from God as a result of fasting.

Scriptures that Speak for Health

Proverbs 3:7, 8 – "Do not be wise in your own eyes; Fear the LORD and turn away from evil. ⁸It will be healing to your body and refreshment to your bones."

Proverbs 17:22 – "A cheerful heart is a good medicine, but a crushed spirit dries up the bones."

Helping With Visiting The Sick As An Outreach

When we are sick or injured, it is always good to know that someone else cares about us and is thinking about us. When visiting the sick or doing any form of ministry, it is good to pray for the person before you arrive at the hospital or their home. One other thing to keep in mind, Proverbs says, "A merry heart does good like a medicine." Not only is this a fact of scripture, but it has scientific evidence to back it up. When we are happy, our bodies release certain hormones that can help speed up the recovery process. Let's make someone happy and healthy! Here are some suggestions of what you can do:

- Take flowers and greeting cards to the sick people in the hospital or convalescent home. When you give flowers to someone, you're simply showing them your depth of love and care that transcends what physical money can do. Online or physical Greeting cards with messages of hope in Christ Jesus can give them another shot at life because the word of God is power, and can heal the sick.
- Find other like-minded people that will partner with you on the same outreach project.
- Send flowers, cards, or food to people who have been hurt or placed in the hospital.

Share Compassion Within the Framework of These Ideas

- Read scripture to the sick; often, seriously ill people are open to listening to the gospel. Refer to the comfort in Christ that is available to them in Christ Jesus.
- If you think the person is open to praying with you, this could be a good way of talking to them about salvation and its benefits. Many times, this can be a quick decision as a person may not know if they will make it out of their sickness. Pray and let the spirit move you in sharing your faith with them in Christ.

Scriptures that Speak for Visitation

Matthew 25:34-36 – "Then the king will say to those on his right, "Come, you who are blessed by my Father, inherit the kingdom prepared for you from the foundation of the world. 35. For I was hungry, and you gave me food, I was thirsty, and you gave me something to drink, I was a stranger, and you invited me in, 36. I was naked, and you gave me clothing, I was sick, and you took care of me, I was in prison, and you visited me."

Helping With The Handicapped As An Outreach

Throughout His ministry, Jesus went about and miraculously healed many people – the sick, the dying, and the physically disabled. Imagine yourself as the extended hand of Jesus as he did many years ago touching, reaching out to the crippled and the afflicted. Here are some outreach suggestions for helping the disabled.

- People with handicaps or disabilities, deserve to live their lives in comfort. They need to be loved and cared for without hesitation because going by their daily activities could be challenging. You can minister to them by becoming a driver for an organization that helps disabled citizens.
- You can also coordinate a fund-raiser to get a person a better wheelchair or vehicle with handicapped access, volunteer as a mentor or caregiver for a disabled person, or even write or read letters for them.

Share Compassion Within the Framework of These Ideas

- Look for another handicapped Christian to help share the ministry of Christ with this person. Let them know that you are helping out because Christ told us to reach out to people, to give a helping hand.
- Always be a salesperson for Christ, selling the benefits of being a Christian, and be concerned about our after reward, which is in heaven. Ensure you give books written by Christians who are handicapped.

Scriptures that Speak for Handicap

Acts 3:6 – "Now a man who was lame from birth was being carried to the temple gate called Beautiful, where he was put every day to beg from those going into the temple courts. When he saw Peter and John about to enter, he asked them for money. Peter looked straight at him, as did John. Then Peter said, "Look at us!" So the man gave them his attention, expecting to get something from them. Then Peter said, "Silver or gold I do not have, but what I do have I give you. In the name of Jesus Christ of Nazareth, walk."

Helping Those With Substance Abuse As An Outreach

Have you heard the phrase, "The devil made me do it?" This is how people with an addiction problem sometimes feel. Many of them would like to stop, but they don't know how to do it. The human body doesn't work like that. It takes a miracle from God, and the power from above to be able to break addiction problems. Pray and help a person to call upon God for deliverance.

Here are some other ways to help people with addictions:

- People with substance abuse need close monitoring and attention before they can escape this devil-ensnared route. You can minister to them by encouraging them to enroll in a support group, and offer to go to a support group meeting with them.
- need to understand that giving money to these people at this stage might not help with their associating problems; the best you can do is to provide them with spiritual and emotional support.
- You can also try to engage them in some kind of health practice and then try to bring up a heart-to-heart conversation about the issue and how they can fair better in the situation.

Share Compassion Within the Framework of These Ideas

- Pray and fast before having your meetings with them. Have a personal Bible study with the person in question, and give them study scriptures that address substance abuse while showing them God's will for their lives.
- Invite them to a church that offers a biblically focused substance abuse class, and help them to look toward the future, their health, and how important their body is to God as the temple of Christ.

Scriptures that Speak for Substance Abuse

Ephesians 5:18-20 – "And do not get drunk with wine, for that is dissipation, but be filled with the Spirit, 19. speaking to one another in psalms and hymns and spiritual songs, singing and making melody with your heart to the Lord, 20. always giving thanks for all things in the name of our Lord Jesus Christ to God, even the Father; and be subject to one another in the fear of Christ."

Romans 13:13-14 – "Let us behave properly as in the day, not in carousing and drunkenness, not in sexual promiscuity and sensuality, not in strife and jealousy. 14. But put on the Lord Jesus Christ, and make no provision for the flesh in regard to its lusts."

Helping With Those in Shelters As An Outreach

Shelter ministry focuses on tools to use when reaching out to the people in shelters. It is important to pray for the Lord's leading and direction on which one you should use. Survey the shelter to see what the needs are, and then prepare a plan that will allow you to use your talents for God's glory in this ministry. Here are some other suggestions:

- Help people find jobs; when people can work, their shelter will be literally taken care of. Cook meals for those living in a shelter and play them inspirational music that can edify their souls. Give them inspirational online sites or apps with scripture verses that can assure their place in Christ Jesus.
- Share with them about the path and process to achieving success, and on how to become stabilized. Become a mentor to a person who enjoys reading, help to create a library on health and other topics.
- Use the skills you have for training, create tutor guides for children in the shelter. Create a play area for children and read stories to them.

Share Compassion Within the Framework of These Ideas

- You can start by setting a target of 2-3 people you want to talk to per week and tell them about the Lord and His love. Follow up on this by arranging rides to take them to churches in the area for Sunday morning worship, and don't forget to give them Christian material that talks about the love of Christ.
- If you know Christian businesses that may need a little work and someone from the shelter is willing to do the job, this could be an excellent time for sharing the message of the Lord.

Scriptures that Speak for Shelter

Isaiah 25:4 – "You have been a refuge for the poor, a refuge for the needy in his distress, a shelter from the storm and a shade from the heat."

Isaiah 58:7, 8 – "Is it not to divide your bread with the hungry and bring the homeless poor into the house; when you see the naked, to cover him; and not to hide yourself from your own flesh? 8. Then your light will break out like the dawn, and your recovery will speedily spring forth;

and your righteousness will go before you; the glory of the LORD will be your rear guard."

Helping With Children As An Outreach

"Children are a blessing from the Lord," as Psalms 127 says. The Lord said, "Unless we come as little children, we can't receive the kingdom of heaven." When reaching out to children, keep in mind that they are a blessing to Him, and even more so when they know the Father and want to serve Him. How can you help with this ministry?

- The best way to build a God-solid foundation for our children is to start teaching them the way of the Lord at the early stages of their lives. Children learn quickly from what they hear, see or participate in, and a great way to minister in this outreach is to start planning to have a kids' day at your home. Treat them to nice Christian folktales and story time.
- You can also invite children over and have a game night at your home under your supervision or any other trusted adults available. Another idea is to host a movie night that talks about the love of God once a month or a week in your home.
- Children love Christmas, and this should be an opportunity to tell them about the love and birth of Christ. You can organize a children's concert for Christmas, and this should depict why Christ loves them.

Share Compassion Within the Framework of These Ideas

- At your movie night, make your first or second movie, a Christian video. When you have story time, always include tales about Christianity in the four or five books you are reading.

- A children's day at your house is a great time to develop a good relationship with a parent. Share your experience about personal growth and how your child is growing spiritually.

Scriptures that Speak for Children

Matthew 21:15-16 – "But when the chief priests and the scribes saw the wonderful things that He had done, and the children who were shouting in the temple, "Hosanna to the Son of David," they became indignant and said to Him, 16. "Do You hear what these *children* are saying?" And Jesus said to them, "Yes; have you never read, 'OUT OF THE MOUTH OF INFANTS AND NURSING BABIES YOU HAVE PREPARED PRAISE FOR YOURSELF'?"

Luke18:15-17 – "And they were bringing even their babies to Him so that He would touch them, but when the disciples saw it, they *began* rebuking them. [16.] But Jesus called for them, saying, "Permit the children to come to Me, and do not hinder them, for the kingdom of God belongs to such as these. 17. "Truly I say to you, whoever does not receive the kingdom of God like a child will not enter it *at all*."

Helping Relatives As An Outreach

Regarding family members, God has given us specific instructions in Isaiah 58:7 – "Do not turn your back on your own flesh and blood." Instead, we need to pray for God's leading on how to approach a relative. Witnessing to family members can often be very difficult because they often see us in a different light than others; thus, they tend to remember many things about us from the past. Sometimes, this may become a stumbling block for them. When you are considering this form of outreach, ensure you pray for the spirit of God to use you in the most creative possible way to reach them with the gospel. Here are some methods of family outreach you can adopt:

- Family is all that matters, and we must find a way of keeping them in harmony while trailing their eyes to the Lord's way. A great way to start is to create a day and dedicate it as fun-filled for the family; do something with them like fishing, golf, shopping, etc.
- You can also organize a family picnic and offer to take them out for dinner, lunch, or breakfast.
- You can send them a card or a gift for their birthday along with scripture to encourage them on how special they are and show concern about their future or that of their children.

Share Compassion Within the Framework of These Ideas

- Find Scriptures that support subjects you both are passionate about, and discuss them wholeheartedly.
- Invite them to church or any special Christian events, and send them online material with Christian messages of hope and support.

Scriptures that Speak for Family

I Timothy 5:4 – "...should learn first of all to put their religion into practice by caring for their own family and so repaying their parents and grandparents, for this is pleasing to God."

1 Timothy 5:8 – "Anyone who does not provide for their relatives, and especially for their own household, has denied the faith and is worse than an unbeliever."

Helping The Convalescent & Hospitals As An Outreach

Convalescent and hospital outreach programs are similar to one another, and you can use some of the same tips to reach out to the people in these institutions. However, there are some fundamental differences, which allow for different ministry opportunities. The hospital offers more one-on-one ministry time, while the convalescent home can be organized into a group outreach setting. This will allow you to put on group activities and projects, such as sing-alongs or crafts. Like the hospital, the convalescent outreach will also allow for one-on-one ministry opportunities. How can you come onboard?

- Take flowers, to a room, or a person in dire need of love and attention. You can also give greeting cards or books if the person can focus enough to read, and endeavor to read to those who cannot.
- Use skills such as storytelling, letter reading, or playing music when you visit and volunteer wherever your help is needed.

Share Compassion Within the Framework of These Ideas

- Sharing the gospel is always easier when the person is confined. Be sensitive and ask questions about their likes and dislikes to determine how best to share the gospel with them.
- You can give an online playlist on good teaching of the Bible for them to listen to.

Scriptures that Speak for Convalescent & Hospital

Isaiah 35:3-5 – "Encourage the exhausted, and strengthen the feeble. 4. Say to those with anxious heart, "Take courage, fear not. Behold, your God will come *with* vengeance; the recompense of God will come, but He will save you. 5. Then the eyes of the blind will be opened and the ears of the deaf will be unstopped."

Helping With Pregnant Teens As An Outreach

Just like the woman by the well, pregnant teens are often quickly judged by many. But the scriptures say, "For all have sinned and fall short of the glory of God," (Romans 3:23). He has given us mercy through Jesus Christ. Pregnant teens and the children they are carrying are both loved by God. Pray for them as the love of God works through you, gives help, and leads them to Christ. Here are a few examples of how you can minister to pregnant teens. (This should be done by women.)

- Teens sometimes make mistakes in the early stages of their lives, and that shouldn't be the end of their existence. All we have to do is rally around them when such mistakes happen and give them guidance to hope in Christ Jesus. You can start ministering to them by calling to see how things are going with them and buy clothes for their newborn.
- You can also work as a volunteer at a pregnancy center, become a mentor for a young girl; meet with her, offer support and compassion that will help her to become more productive.
- You can also offer to give her a ride to her doctor's appointment, and invite her to other Christian-sponsored young-pregnant moms groups that will help her to understand how to deal with her body transformation.

Share Compassion Within the Framework of These Ideas

- Talk about the health of the mom, baby, and her spiritual health through a prosperous future with Jesus. Invite her to a church with a good children's ministry.
- Meet with her to discuss her need to continue her education and to develop skills for her future. Share the gospel and how it addresses the plan and principles of a healthy, moral life.

Scriptures that Speak for the Pregnant Teens

John 8:3-11 – "The scribes and the Pharisees brought a woman caught in adultery, 4. and having set her in the center *of the court,* they said to Him,

"Teacher, this woman has been caught in adultery, in the very act. Now 5. in the Law Moses commanded us to stone such women; what then do You say?" 6. They were saying this, testing Him, so that they might have grounds for accusing Him. But Jesus stooped down and with His finger wrote on the ground. 7. But when they persisted in asking Him, He straightened up, and said to them, "He who is without sin among you, let him *be the* first to throw a stone at her." 8. Again He stooped down and wrote on the ground. 9. When they heard it, they *began* to go out one by one, beginning with the older ones, and He was left alone, and the woman, where she was, in the center *of the court*. Straightening up, 10. Jesus said to her, "Woman, where are they? Did no one condemn you?" She said, 11. "No one, Lord." And Jesus said, "I do not condemn you, either. Go. From now on sin no more."

Helping With Parent Development As An Outreach

Parenting can be challenging, even for the best of parents. There are many books on parenting, but even those books cannot discuss every problem that a parent is likely to encounter. Sometimes it can be helpful to have a real person we can discuss certain issues with. Ideas and personal experience can go a long way. This could be a great time to share some of your experiences and some good ideas that you have. Give it your best, and God will give you the wisdom to share some of those good ideas. Who knows, you may also have an opportunity to share your faith in the Lord. How can you help?

- Parenting is like gardening; we must do everything to keep them safe from predators and other forms of hazards. With parenting, our children, like plants need food, sun and a place to grow. Children thrive best when they are eating properly, sleeping adequately, getting outside in nature and feeling safe in their homes. Children also need to know they are loved and cared for. To get help in this area, you can go to the kids' section in a book store, meet parents, and share ideas on child-rearing. You can also get involved in the school your child attends, and join the P.T.A. Another to this approach is to start a parent club and do various projects that will improve your child's total wellbeing.

Share Compassion Within the Framework of These Ideas

- Invite a parent to your church, to a children's event, a play, or a parenting workshop, and discuss your aspirations for their children and what will happen with our todays youth if these little children are not rooted in God's words.
- Within a parent club, invite a parent out for coffee or over for lunch. At that point, Christ can make a difference in their lives.

Scriptures that Speak for Parent Development

Proverbs 22:6 – "Start children off on the way they should go, and even when they are old they will not turn from it."

2 Corinthians 12:14 – "...After all, children should not have to save up for their parents, but parents for their children."

Ephesians 6:4 – "Fathers, do not exasperate your children; instead, bring them up in the training and instruction of the Lord."

Helping With The Fatherless/ Motherless As An Outreach

Think about being without a mother or a father as a little child. Some of us can't imagine it, but God hurts when one of these little ones has lost either a father or a mother, or both. When dealing with this ministry, imagine how it would feel to be one of these little ones. Think about what kinds of activities might help that child, and how you might help nurture a relationship with Christ. Having a calling for the fatherless and motherless ministry? Here is how you can help:

- There are so many things we can do for the motherless and fatherless orphans to keep them off the street and help them align their God-given potentials. One of those things is to be a mentor for a child who has lost a parent by paying for or giving lessons in computers, music, art, or a sport, etc.
- You can also be a sponsor for a healthy organization that caters to children.

Share Compassion Within the Framework of These Ideas

- Find other Christian children who have the ability to share their faith with this child, and invite them to a spirit filled youth group.
- You can also help them to raise money or help pay their way to go on trips with the youth group.

Scriptures that Speak for the Fatherless/Motherless

James 1:27 – "Religion that God our Father accepts as pure and faultless is this: to look after orphans and widows in their distress and to keep oneself from being polluted by the world."

Psalm 68:5 – "A father to the fatherless, a defender of widows, is God in his holy dwelling. God sets the lonely in families, he leads forth the prisoners with singing: but the rebellious live in a sun-scorched land."

Conclusion – We Are Called For Good Works

When we talk about God's salvation to mankind, what comes to mind is He saved us - you and me. Salvation is not all about going to Heaven. We cannot say we are saved, and that is the only key. Jesus always tells those he delivered, "Go sin no more." This means go and do what I do, which implies that being saved does not mean we are eligible for Heaven, you cannot be a true believer if you do not follow the footsteps of the Master. What I want us to understand here is that claiming and believing Christ without following His teachings, instructions, and governing of life with these systems cannot get us to Heaven. Now, what is the purpose of this salvation? Why has God saved us? The answer is not to far from everything that this book has made known to us. If we look at the book of Ephesians 2:10, Paul says, "For we are God's workmanship, created in Christ Jesus, to do good works, which God prepared in advance for us to do."

Let us examine this statement and see how outreach is very important in our lives. When Paul says, "We are the workmanship…" he refers to us as believers. True believers are God's workmanship. His project. Created in Christ, the word tells us that we were all sinners, dead, but Jesus came to erase all that. He came to wash our sins and give us a new life in the spirit. Paul says, "…to do good works." Now, this answers the question; purpose of salvation. Not only is our salvation for enjoying Heaven on our last day on earth but also doing good work before our last day.

Moreover, we can never do this good work when we are in Heaven but only when we are on earth, meaning now. In other words, good work has become our salvation, our privilege, God's blessing, and Heaven becomes an extension of God's grace after good works have been done. And this is why we are saved. Showing love, helping the needy, and doing all that is good is what describes the heart, soul, and life of a Christian. From this book, we can understand that good works are not exclusive for our family, friends, pregnancy centers, or bible mission stores; instead, it is something that can be established in all areas of life. There are a lot of people out there, fortunate or unfortunate that need our help. Many people get it wrong when they think, "This is my life; I can do what I want." Some will say, "I do not steal or kill. I helped that old lady cross the road." Yes, this is good but it goes beyond that. Below you will see how outreach is a form of good works.

1. Good works comes from faith. Faith connects us to Christ Jesus when we believe in Him; He lives in us, and as He dwells in us, he uses us to do good work, making us His instruments. This is equivalent to being His workmanship, and as I stated earlier, only those who have faith in God can give without thinking of how much resources they have left.
2. Good works as a form of outreach conforms with the law of God. If we look at the verses underneath each outreach, we see that all are backed by the Holy Book, most of which are instructions for us as true believers.
3. Good works as a form of outreach glorifies God. They are not done for us to be honored; rather, for those that we help and serve to glorify and see Him as God; also for them to see His reign and believe that He sent His Son to die for us all.

Can we all say that we are doing these good works? Or admit that we have such faith and that our lives are bounded by the law of God? Having read this book, we may not be able to do all, but it doesn't mean that we cannot do some; this is because there are different services in the kingdom of God. However, we are gifted in different ways, but one thing we must keep in mind is that we are all called to serve.

Some may wonder how this is possible because you feel you are unworthy of these tasks, or you do not see yourself fit to do these things. Well, Paul ended his statement with "..... which God prepared in advance for us to do." I will use the life of the Israelites to explain this portion. If we look at the Old Testament from the book of Exodus to Joshua, we are told of the Israelites journey. In Deuteronomy 7, the Lord said to Israel that He will lead them to the Promise Land, that this was His plan for them. The bible also tells us that there were many strong nations like Jericho, Amorites, Hivites, and Girgashites in the land of Canaan. Nations with thousands of soldiers and this made the Israelites scared. But the Lord said to them, "......from all the people on the earth I have chosen you to be My own special people."

God also told them not to fear that He would drive out seven nations on their behalf. Now, this explains *"pre-destiny."* We all have been predestined for good works, so why fear? Why doubt? Why relent? Why feel unworthy? Instead, let us all go out and do what the Lord has planned in advance for us, let us do it with confidence and joy. Because we have been saved and thus, we have been given a task – one that has been prepared for us, which means all we can do is to go out and do them. He who has planned this will use us to make it work, and so if we break Ephesians 2:10 in four lines, this is what we get;

1. We are His workmanship equals YOU
2. Created in Christ Jesus equals belonging to Jesus and delivered by the Holy Spirit
3. To do good works equals our salvation, which is divided into two. Firstly, good works and secondly, the grace of Heaven.
4. Which God prepared in advance for us equals destiny, purpose, task, also, seen as God's plan for us.

With this, I encourage us all to go and do this work. This book has shown us various ways that we can help. God is calling every one of us, let us all heed to this call, and we, in turn, shall be blessed abundantly by our Heavenly Father, in Jesus' Name, Amen.

Isaiah 58 New International Version (NIV)

True Fasting

58
"Shout it aloud, do not hold back.
 Raise your voice like a trumpet.
Declare to my people their rebellion
 and to the descendants of Jacob their sins.

2
For day after day they seek me out;
 they seem eager to know my ways,
as if they were a nation that does what is right
 and has not forsaken the commands of its God.
They ask me for just decisions
 and seem eager for God to come near them.

3
'Why have we fasted,' they say,
 'and you have not seen it?
Why have we humbled ourselves,
 and you have not noticed?'
"Yet on the day of your fasting, you do as you please
 and exploit all your workers.

4
Your fasting ends in quarreling and strife,
 and in striking each other with wicked fists.
You cannot fast as you do today
 and expect your voice to be heard on high.

5
Is this the kind of fast I have chosen,
    only a day for people to humble themselves?
Is it only for bowing one's head like a reed
    and for lying in sackcloth and ashes?
Is that what you call a fast,
    a day acceptable to the Lord?

6
"Is not this the kind of fasting I have chosen:
to loose the chains of injustice
    and untie the cords of the yoke,
to set the oppressed free
    and break every yoke?

7
Is it not to share your food with the hungry
    and to provide the poor wanderer with shelter—
when you see the naked, to clothe them,
    and not to turn away from your own flesh and blood?

8
Then your light will break forth like the dawn,
    and your healing will quickly appear;
then your righteousness[a] will go before you,
    and the glory of the Lord will be your rear guard.

9
Then you will call, and the Lord will answer;
    you will cry for help, and he will say: Here am I.
"If you do away with the yoke of oppression,
    with the pointing finger and malicious talk,

10
and if you spend yourselves in behalf of the hungry
    and satisfy the needs of the oppressed,
then your light will rise in the darkness,
    and your night will become like the noonday.
11
The Lord will guide you always;
    he will satisfy your needs in a sun-scorched land
    and will strengthen your frame.
You will be like a well-watered garden,
    like a spring whose waters never fail.
12
Your people will rebuild the ancient ruins
    and will raise up the age-old foundations;
you will be called Repairer of Broken Walls,
    Restorer of Streets with Dwellings.
13
"If you keep your feet from breaking the Sabbath
    and from doing as you please on my holy day,
if you call the Sabbath a delight
    and the Lord's holy day honorable,
and if you honor it by not going your own way
    and not doing as you please or speaking idle words,
14
then you will find your joy in the Lord,
    and I will cause you to ride in triumph on the heights of the land
    and to feast on the inheritance of your father Jacob."
For the mouth of the Lord has spoken.

Community Outreach Organizations to Work With

Handicap Outreach	Vocational Rehabilitation
Letter Writing Outreach	Local Churches
Tutoring Outreach	Local Libraries and Schools
Elderly Outreach	Local Senior Organizations
Food Outreach	Food Banks
Visiting the Sick Outreach	Local Hospitals
Fatherless Outreach	Volunteer Centers
Telephone Outreach	Local Churches
Next-door Neighbor Outreach	Local Churches
Grief Outreach	Hospice Cancer Support
Newborn Outreach	Local Hospitals
Substance Abuse Outreach	Local Treatment Centers
College and School Outreach	Your Local Schools
Internet Outreach	Your Computer or Library
Health & Mental Health Outreach	Salvation Army
Music Outreach	Local Concert Halls
Media Outreach	Newspapers, TV, Radio, Internet
Street Outreach	Local Churches
Sports Outreach	Local Sports Teams
Parent Development Outreach	Local Churches
Jail/Prison Outreach	City Team Ministry, Match One
Homeless Outreach	Local Shelters, Salvation Army, etc.

Widow Outreach..Local Churches
Children's Outreach..........................YMCA, Scouts, Little League, etc.
Relative Outreach ....YMCA, Scouts, Little League, etc.
Business Outreach..Businessmen Fellowship
Job Outreach.. Your Workplace
Pregnant Teen Outreach ....Crisis Pregnancy Center
Employee Outreach...Your Employees/Coworkers

Outreach Contact List

NAME _____
ADDRESS _____
CITY/STATE / ZIP _____
PHONE _____
E-MAIL _____

NAME _____
ADDRESS _____
CITY/STATE / ZIP _____
PHONE _____
E-MAIL _____

NAME _____
ADDRESS _____
CITY/STATE / ZIP _____
PHONE _____
E-MAIL _____

NAME _____
ADDRESS _____
CITY/STATE / ZIP _____
PHONE _____
E-MAIL _____

NAME _____
ADDRESS _____
CITY/STATE / ZIP _____
PHONE _____
E-MAIL _____

NAME _____
ADDRESS _____
CITY/STATE / ZIP _____
PHONE _____
E-MAIL _____

NAME _____
ADDRESS _____
CITY/STATE / ZIP _____
PHONE _____
E-MAIL _____

NAME _____
ADDRESS _____
CITY/STATE / ZIP _____
PHONE _____
E-MAIL _____

Directory of Local Churches

NAME _____   NAME _____
PASTOR _____   PASTOR _____
ADDRESS _____   ADDRESS _____
CITY/STATE / ZIP _____   CITY/STATE / ZIP _____
PHONE _____   PHONE _____
E-MAIL/WEBSITE _____   E-MAIL/WEBSITE _____
IDEA OF CHURCH TYPE _____   IDEA OF CHURCH TYPE _____

NAME _____   NAME _____
PASTOR _____   PASTOR _____
ADDRESS _____   ADDRESS _____
CITY/STATE / ZIP _____   CITY/STATE / ZIP _____
PHONE _____   PHONE _____
E-MAIL/WEBSITE _____   E-MAIL/WEBSITE _____
IDEA OF CHURCH TYPE _____   IDEA OF CHURCH TYPE _____

NAME _____   NAME _____
PASTOR _____   PASTOR _____
ADDRESS _____   ADDRESS _____
CITY/STATE / ZIP _____   CITY/STATE / ZIP _____
PHONE _____   PHONE _____
E-MAIL/WEBSITE _____   E-MAIL/WEBSITE _____
IDEA OF CHURCH TYPE _____   IDEA OF CHURCH TYPE _____

Prayer Requests

NAME _____ PHONE _____
PRAYER NEED _____
_____

NAME _____ PHONE _____
PRAYER NEED _____
_____

NAME _____ PHONE _____
PRAYER NEED _____
_____

NAME _____ PHONE _____
PRAYER NEED _____
_____

NAME _____ PHONE _____
PRAYER NEED _____
_____

How to guide people in Prayer when they are ready to accept Christ

A simple prayer...

When a new believer decides to accept Jesus into his or her heart, there are no magic formulas that need to be followed, no rituals that the individual needs to perform. Saying a simple heart-felt prayer is all that one needs to do to accept the love of Christ. Following is one version of this simple prayer that one can say. Either you can say this prayer with someone who is seeking Jesus, or a person may say this prayer on their own.

Dear God, I ask you to come into my heart. Please forgive me for my sins. I accept you, Jesus, into my heart, as my personal savior.

It's Done!

Once a person receives Christ, keep him or her in your prayer list, praying for God's strength to keep them. Be sure to give them as much support as possible.

Things you can do to support a new convert:

1. Give them a Bible and direct them in studying the word of God.
2. Take them to church or a Bible study, or recommend a church.

3. Encourage them to get baptized and educate them on the process.
4. REJOICE IN THE LORD FOR ANOTHER SOUL IN THE KINGDOM OF GOD!
5. For additional material, see your church or Christian book store.

How to guide people in Prayer when they are ready to accept Christ

Supporting scripture for new Christians

Romans 10:8-11 – "The word is near you, it is in your mouth and in your heart" that is, the word of faith we are proclaiming: 9. That if you confess with your mouth, "Jesus is Lord," and believe in your heart that God raised him from the dead, you will be saved. 10. For it is with your heart that you believe and are justifiedfied, and with your mouth that you confess and are saved. 11. As the scripture says, "Anyone who trusts in him will never be put to shame."

Matthew 10:32 – ""Therefore everyone who confesses Me before men, I will also confess him before My Father who is in heaven. "But whoever denies Me before men, I will also deny him before My Father who is in heaven."

Useful Scriptures for Outreach

Homeless Outreach

Matthew 25:35-40 "For I was hungry, and you gave Me *something* to eat; I was thirsty, and you gave Me *something* to drink; I was a stranger, and you invited Me in; [36] naked, and you clothed Me; I was sick, and you visited Me; I was in prison, and you came to Me.' [37] "Then the righteous will answer Him, 'Lord, when did we see You hungry, and feed You, or thirsty, and give You *something* to drink? [38] 'And when did we see You a stranger, and invite You in, or naked, and clothe You? [39] 'When did we see You sick, or in prison, and come to You?' [40] "The King will answer and say to them, 'Truly I say to you, to the extent that you did it to one of these brothers of Mine, *even* the least *of them,* you did it to Me."

Isaiah 58:7 – "Is it not to share your food with the hungry and to provide the poor wanderer with shelter-- when you see the naked, to clothe them, and not to turn away from your own flesh and blood?"

Widows Outreach

James 1:27 – "Religion that God our Father accepts as pure and faultless is this: to look after orphans and widows in their distress and to keep oneself from being polluted by the world."

Food Outreach

James 2:15-17 – " If a brother or sister is without clothing and in need of daily food, 16. and one of you says to them, "Go in peace, be warmed and be filled," and yet you do not give them what is necessary for *their* body, what use is that? 17. Even so faith, if it has no works, is dead, *being* by itself."

Psalm 136:25 – "To the one who gives food to all living things, for his loyal love endures. Give thanks to the God of heaven. His love endures forever."

School/Tutoring Outreach

1 Corinthians 4:16-21 – "Therefore I exhort you, be imitators of me. [17] For this reason I have sent to you Timothy, who is my beloved and faithful child in the Lord, and he will remind you of my ways which are in Christ, just as I teach everywhere in every church. [18] Now some have become arrogant, as though I were not coming to you. [19] But I will come to you soon, if the Lord wills, and I shall find out, not the words of those who are arrogant but their power. [20] For the kingdom of God does not consist in words but in power. [21] What do you desire? Shall I come to you with a rod, or with love and a spirit of gentleness?"

Psalm 32:8 – "I will instruct you and teach you in the way you should go; I will counsel you with my loving eye on you."

College Outreach

Ephesians 4:11-13 – 'And He gave some *as* apostles, and some *as* prophets, and some *as* evangelists, and some *as* pastors and teachers, 12. for the equipping of the saints for the work of service, to the building up of the body of Christ; 13. until we all attain to the unity of the faith, and of the knowledge of the Son of God, to a mature man, to the measure of the stature which belongs to the fullness of Christ.'

Elderly Outreach

Psalm 71:8-9 – "My mouth is filled with Your praise and with Your glory all day long. 9. Do not cast me off in the time of old age; do not forsake me when my strength fails."

Telephone Outreach

1 Peter 4:11 – "If anyone speaks, they should do so as one who speaks the very words of God. If anyone serves, they should do so with the strength God provides, so that in all things God may be praised through Jesus Christ. To him be the glory and the power for ever and ever. Amen."

Colossians 4:6 – "Let your conversation be always full of grace, seasoned with salt, so that you may know how to answer everyone."

Grief Outreach

Psalm 121:1-2 – "I will lift up my eyes to the mountains; From where shall my help come? 2. My help *comes* from the LORD, Who made heaven and earth!"

Job/Employee Outreach

Matthew 5:13-14 – " You are the salt of the earth; but if the salt has become tasteless, how can it be made salty *again?* It is no longer good for anything, except to be thrown out and trampled under-foot by men. 14. You are the light of the world. A city set on a hill cannot be hidden."

Ephesians 4:28 – "…he must work, doing something useful with their own hands, that they may have something to share with those in need."

Business Outreach

I Corinthians 3:6-9 – "I planted, Apollos watered, but God was causing the growth. 7. So then neither the one who plants nor the one who waters is anything, but God who causes the growth. 8. Now he who plants and he who waters are one; but each will receive his own reward according to his own labor. 9. For we are God's fellow workers; you are God's field, God's building."

Jail Outreach

Matthew 25:35-36 – "For I was hungry, and you gave me food, I was thirsty, and you gave me something to drink, I was a stranger, and you invited me in, 36. I was naked, and you gave me clothing, I was sick, and you took care of me, I was in prison, and you visited me."

Street Outreach

Matthew 22:9,10 – "Go therefore to the main highways, and as many as you find *there,* invite to the wedding feast.' 10. Those slaves went out into the streets and gathered together all they found, both evil and good; and the wedding hall was filled with dinner guests."

Luke 14:23 – "Then the master told his servant, 'Go out to the roads and country lanes and compel them to come in, so that my house will be full."

Activate God's Blessings

Next Door Neighbor Outreach

Matthew 5:43-45 – "You have heard that it was said, 'YOU SHALL LOVE YOUR NEIGHBOR and hate your enemy.' 44. But I say to you, love your enemies and pray for those who persecute you, so 45. that you may be sons of your Father who is in heaven; for He causes His sun to rise on *the* evil and *the* good, and sends rain on *the* righteous and *the* unrighteous."

Letter Writing Outreach

1 Corinthians 1:1-3 – "Paul, called *as* an apostle of Jesus Christ by the will of God, and Sosthenes our brother, 2. to the church of God which is at Corinth, to those who have been sanctified in Christ Jesus, saints by calling, with all who in every place call on the name of our Lord Jesus Christ, their *Lord* and ours: 3. Grace to you and peace from God our Father and the Lord Jesus Christ!"

Sports Outreach

Hebrews 12:1- 2 – " Therefore, since we have so great a cloud of witnesses surrounding us, let us also lay aside every encumbrance and the sin which so easily entangles us, and let us run with endurance the race that is set before us, 2. fixing our eyes on Jesus, the author and perfecter of faith, who for the joy set before Him endured the cross, despising the shame, and has sat down at the right hand of the throne of God."

Music Outreach

I Samuel 16 14-23 – "Now the Spirit of the LORD departed from Saul, and an evil spirit from the LORD terrorized him. [15]Saul's servants then said to him, "Behold now, an evil spirit from God is terrorizing you. [16]"Let our lord now command your servants who are before you. Let them seek a man who is a skillful player on the harp; and it shall come about when the evil spirit from God is on you, that he shall play *the harp* with his hand, and you will be well." [17]So Saul said to his servants, "Provide for me now a man who can play well and bring *him* to me." [18]Then one of the young men said, "Behold, I have seen a son of Jesse the Bethlehemite who is a skillful musician, a mighty man of valor, a warrior, one prudent in speech, and a handsome man; and the LORD is with him." [19]So Saul sent messengers to Jesse and said, "Send me your son David who is with the flock." [20]Jesse took a donkey *loaded with* bread and a jug of wine and a young goat, and sent *them* to Saul by David his son. [21] Then David came to Saul and attended him; and Saul loved him greatly, and he became his armor bearer. [22] Saul sent to Jesse, saying, "Let David now stand before me, for he has found favor in my sight." [23] So it came about whenever the *evil* spirit from God came to Saul, David would take the harp and play *it* with his hand; and Saul would be refreshed and be well, and the evil spirit would depart from him."

Media Outreach

Matthew 9:35-38 – 'Jesus was going through all the cities and villages, teaching in their synagogues and proclaiming the gospel of the kingdom, and healing every kind of disease and every kind of sickness. [36] Seeing the people, He felt compassion for them, because they were distressed and dispirited like sheep without a shepherd. [37] Then He said to His disciples, "The harvest is plentiful, but the workers are few. [38] "Therefore beseech the Lord of the harvest to send out workers into His harvest."

Matthew 10:1 – "Jesus called his twelve disciples to him and gave them authority to drive out impure spirits and to heal every disease and sickness."

Internet Outreach

John 5:20 – " For the Father loves the Son and shows him all he does. Yes, and he will show him even greater works than these, so that you will be amazed."

Health Outreach

3 John 1:2 – "Dear friend, I pray that you may enjoy good health and that all may go well with you, even as your soul is getting along well."

Visiting the Sick Outreach

Matthew 25:34-36 – "Then the king will say to those on his right, "Come, you who are blessed by my Father, inherit the kingdom prepared for you from the foundation of the world. 35. For I was hungry, and you gave me food, I was thirsty, and you gave me something to drink, I was a stranger, and you invited me in, 36. I was naked, and you gave me clothing, I was sick, and you took care of me, I was in prison, and you visited me."

Handicapped Outreach

Acts 3:2-6 – "Now a man who was lame from birth was being carried to the temple gate called Beautiful, where he was put every day to beg from those going into the temple courts. ³ When he saw Peter and John about to enter, he asked them for money. ⁴ Peter looked straight at him, as did John. Then Peter said, "Look at us!" ⁵ So the man gave them his attention, expecting to get something from them. ⁶ Then Peter said, "Silver or gold I do not have, but what I do have I give you. In the name of Jesus Christ of Nazareth, walk!"

Substance Abuse Outreach

Galatians 5:19-21 – " Now the deeds of the flesh are evident, which are: immorality, impurity, sensuality, 20. idolatry, sorcery, enmities, strife, jealousy, outbursts of anger, disputes, dissensions, factions, 21. envying, drunkenness, carousing, and things like these, of which I forewarn you, just as I have forewarned you, that those who practice such things will not inherit the kingdom of God."

Ephesians 5:18-21 – "And do not get drunk with wine, for that is dissipation, but be filled with the Spirit, 19. speaking to one another in psalms and hymns and spiritual songs, singing and making melody with your heart to the Lord; 20. always giving thanks for all things in the name of our Lord Jesus Christ to God, even the Father; and be 21. subject to one another in the fear of Christ."

Romans 13:13-14 – "Let us behave properly as in the day, not in carousing and drunkenness, not in sexual promiscuity and sensuality, not in strife and jealousy. 14. But put on the Lord Jesus Christ, and make no provision for the flesh in regard to *its* lusts."

Shelter Outreach

Psalms 5:11 – "But let all who take refuge in you be glad; let them ever sing for joy. Spread your protection over them, that those who love your name may rejoice in you."

Psalm 61:3-5 – "For You have been a refuge for me, a tower of strength against the enemy. 4. Let me dwell in Your tent forever; let me take refuge in the shelter of Your wings. Selah. 5. For You have heard my vows, O God; You have given *me* the inheritance of those who fear Your name."

Convalescent & Hospital Outreach

Isaiah 35:3-5 – "Encourage the exhausted, and strengthen the feeble. 4. Say to those with anxious heart, "Take courage, fear not. Behold, your God will come *with* vengeance; the recompense of God will come, but He will save you. 4. Then the eyes of the blind will be opened and the ears of the deaf will be unstopped."

Parenting Outreach

Proverbs 22:6 –"Start children off on the way they should go, and even when they are old they will not turn from it."

Pregnant Teen Outreach

Psalm 127:3-5 – "Behold, children are a gift of the LORD, the fruit of the womb is a reward. 4. Like arrows in the hand of a warrior, so are the children of one's youth. 5. How blessed is the man whose quiver is full of them; they will not be ashamed; when they speak with their enemies in the gate."

Fatherless Outreach

James 1:27 – "Religion that God our Father accepts as pure and faultless is this: to look after orphans and widows in their distress and to keep oneself from being polluted by the world."

Exodus 22:22 – ""Do not take advantage of the widow or the fatherless."

Children's Outreach

Matthew 21:15, 16 – "But when the chief priests and the scribes saw the wonderful things that He had done, and the children who were shouting in the temple, "Hosanna to the Son of David," they became indignant and said to Him, 16. "Do You hear what these *children* are saying?" And Jesus said to them, "Yes; have you never read, 'OUT OF THE MOUTH OF INFANTS AND NURSING BABIES YOU HAVE PREPARED PRAISE FOR YOURSELF'?"

Luke 18:15 "And they were bringing even their babies to Him so that He would touch them, but when the disciples saw it, they *began* rebuking them,. 16. But Jesus called for them, saying, "Permit the children to come to Me, and do not hinder them, for the kingdom of God belongs to such as these. 17. "Truly I say to you, whoever does not receive the kingdom of God like a child will not enter it *at all*."

Relative Outreach

1 Timothy 5:8 – "Anyone who does not provide for their relatives, and especially for their own household, has denied the faith and is worse than an unbeliever."

Newborn Outreach

Psalm 127:3-5 – "Behold, children are a gift of the LORD, the fruit of the womb is a reward. 4. Like arrows in the hand of a warrior, so are the children of one's youth. 5. How blessed is the man whose quiver is full of them; they will not be ashamed; when they speak with their enemies in the gate."

Personal Outreach Timeline Community Needs

Type of outreach and time/day you will minister					
Homeless Outreach	School/ Tutoring Outreach	Food Outreach	College Outreach	Widow Outreach	Elderly Outreach

Time
Monday
Tuesday
Wednesday
Thursday
Friday
Saturday
Sunday

PERSONAL OUTREACH TIMELINE COMMUNITY NEEDS

Type of outreach and time/day you will minister					
Telephone Outreach	Grief Outreach	Job/ Employee Outreach	Business Outreach	Jail Outreach	Street Outreach

Time
Monday
Tuesday
Wednesday
Thursday
Friday
Saturday
Sunday

Personal Outreach Timeline Community Needs

Type of outreach and time/day you will minister					
Next Door Neighbor Outreach	Letter Writing Outreach	Sports Outreach	Music Outreach	Media Outreach	Internet Outreach

Time
Monday
Tuesday
Wednesday
Thursday
Friday
Saturday
Sunday

Personal Outreach Timeline Community Needs

Type of outreach and time/day you will minister					
Health Outreach	Visiting the Sick Outreach	Handicapped Outreach	Substance Abuse Outreach	Shelter Outreach	Convalescent & Hospital Outreach

Time
Monday
Tuesday
Wednesday
Thursday
Friday
Saturday
Sunday

Personal Outreach Timeline Community Needs

Type of outreach and time/day you will minister						
Parenting Outreach	Pregnant Teen Outreach	Fatherless Outreach	Children's Outreach	Relative's Outreach	Newborn Outreach

Time
Monday
Tuesday
Wednesday
Thursday
Friday
Saturday
Sunday

www.ingramcontent.com/pod-product-compliance
Lightning Source LLC
Chambersburg PA
CBHW071630080526
44588CB00010B/1346